Contents

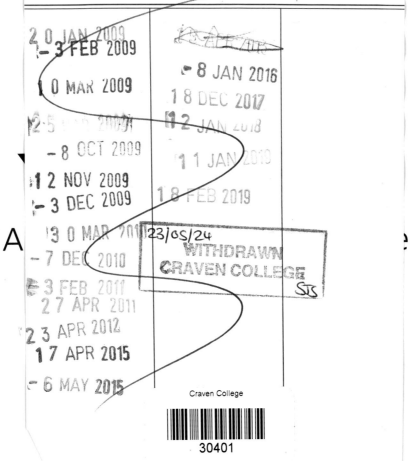

RHP

Russell House Publishing

First published in 2006 by:
Russell House Publishing Ltd.
4 St. George's House
Uplyme Road
Lyme Regis
Dorset DT7 3LS
Tel: 01297-443948
Fax: 01297-442722
e-mail: help@russellhouse.co.uk

A catalogue record for this book is available from the British Library.

British Library Cataloguing-in-publication Data:

ISBN: 978-1-903855-90-4; 1-903855-90-X

Typeset by TW Typesetting, Plymouth, Devon
Printed by Alden Press, Oxford

About Russell House Publishing

RHP is a group of social work, probation, education and youth and community work practitioners and academics working in collaboration with a professional publishing team.

Our aim is to work closely with the field to produce innovative and valuable materials to help managers, trainers, practitioners and students.

We are keen to receive feedback on publications and new ideas for future projects.

For details of our other publications please visit our website or ask us for a catalogue. Contact details are on this page.

Acknowledgements

This book is dedicated to Isobel and Rose for their unswerving belief in me and their constant love and encouragement; and to Timmy for his devotion and unconditional love for Rose.

Steven Walker

This book is also dedicated to Andrew, who has consistently offered love and support and Christopher Luke for giving me the privilege to see the outstanding man he has become.

Christina Thurston

Introduction

Safeguarding children and child protection are too seldom considered to be everybody's business.

(Laming Report, 2003)

In Britain at least one child dies each week as a result of adult cruelty. It has been estimated that about 5,000 minors are involved in prostitution in Britain at any one time. In 2003 there were about 384,200 children in need in England. Of these 69,100 were looked after in state care while the rest were in families or living independently (DfES, 2003a). By the end of 2002, 21 per cent of children in Britain were living in poverty, increasing their risk of neglect (DWP, 2003). One quarter of all rape victims are children. Seventy five per cent of sexually abused children do not tell anyone at the time. Each year about 30,000 children are on child protection registers. Recorded offences of gross indecency with a child more than doubled between 1985–2001 but convictions against perpetrators actually fell from 42 per cent to 19 per cent. Fewer than one in 50 sexual offences results in a conviction. Plus there is still a major shortfall in supervision and treatment of sexual offenders thus reducing the opportunity to lessen re-offending.

This sample of statistics conveys the scale of the problem facing those who care about children's welfare and want to safeguard them. Individual and family level factors have historically dominated the analysis and locus of child protection legislation, policy and practice. With the publication of *Every Child Matters* (DfES, 2003b), The Children Act 2004 and the creation of integrated Children's Trusts there is now an opportunity to ensure that the community level factors inherent in child abuse and neglect are fully considered. There is now a more intensive focus on integrated work in safeguarding children and young people. This means reinforcing the conclusions drawn from evidence that demonstrates that child abuse is *everybody's business*. And this does not just mean every professional working with children but the *whole community* where children and young people live, work, play and are educated.

The police always remind us that they cannot stop crime without the help of the community and it is the same with safeguarding children. An African proverb states that 'It takes a whole village to raise a child', while ancient Maori custom expects whole communities to get involved when a family has a problem. This is not a manifesto against professionalism but an illustration of a neglected area in modern welfare organisation which has lost sight of the fundamentals in our technocratic and bureaucracy driven culture. Your task is to find innovative ways to engage communities in safeguarding children by encouraging and enhancing people's protective instincts.

Who this book is for

This book aims to provide a resource for practitioners in a variety of community contexts, in voluntary or statutory agencies, who may encounter situations where concerns are expressed about the welfare and safety of a child or young person.

This could be in child protection, primary care, youth offending teams, family support, looked after children, youth work, paediatric nursing, fostering and adoption, education, probation, and child and adolescent mental health services. The guide aspires to provide a foundation of contemporary knowledge, research, innovative ideas and practical guidance that will offer you support. It is written within the context of new government guidelines and legislation following the murder of Victoria Climbié, Jessica Chapman and Holly Wells. The accessible format is designed to create the basis for informed, reflective, confident practice. It will help your individual study, teambuilding exercises and inter-agency training.

Enduring solutions

The government response to recent cases of child deaths where public services are involved it should be remembered, is a political reaction identical to previous occasions when children have died and immediate answers are sought. Instead of dealing with symptoms and searching for scapegoats in this guide we aspire to tackle causes and look for enduring solutions to the unacceptable scourge of child abuse and neglect. Prevention is better than cure so we have tried to include ideas and resources for staff trying to minimise the risk of child abuse in the first place as well as clarity where swift action needs to proceed in child protection cases. Supporting families and vulnerable parents needs to synchronise with child protection agency procedures where children are perceived to be at risk of harm.

The disproportionate numbers of poor families subject to investigation and surveillance is a reminder that safeguarding children can only be as effective as the government's commitment to reducing economic inequality and social exclusion. These figures illustrate the importance of acknowledging the multiple disadvantages experienced by many families where intolerable stress places some children and young people at increased risk of abuse. The bias in official statistics also conspires to mask child abuse where it can be skilfully hidden behind the façade of middle class respectability and material wealth (DoH, 2002; NCH, 2000).

England, Scotland, Wales and Northern Ireland

Within Britain there is much diversity in the legislative and governmental guidance for safeguarding children and young people. This text generally is based on English law for reasons of space and the avoidance of confusion. The Scottish system operates under its own legal system and system of guidance, while in Northern Ireland the health and social services boards make up a very different organisational context for child protection work. The devolved national assemblies in Scotland and Wales further add to this diversity. However the book contents have been adapted and designed to provide significant learning opportunities for practitioners in all the constituent countries of the United Kingdom who will find much of value here.

Content of guide

The guide is designed as a practical manual for use by busy practitioners, trainers and professional education providers requiring evidence-based knowledge and guidance to enable staff to engage with children, adolescents, young people and their families in a supportive context.

It aims to help you articulate with the needs and agenda of children and young people whose safety is causing concern. The 36 activities are designed to stimulate your reflective capacity and together with the practice guidance, offer you resources to bring to bear on the difficulties faced by your clients, service users, students or patients. (They are reproduced at the back of the book for ease of photocopying.) This book covers the wider policy and legal context of safeguarding children and young people and how services for this group of young people are organised and delivered.

Working in the field of safeguarding children and young people is an awesome undertaking. It covers the majority of the most intense and rapidly changing periods of human growth and development, within which are laid the foundations for much of what will transpire in the rest of a person's life. Your contribution is therefore crucial bringing as it does a professional dimension to a child or young person's experience at a time when effective intervention can make a difference for the present and their future. We have sought to provide a varied menu to choose from of accessible and useful resources and information gleaned from contemporary sources of evidence-based literature and quality research, as well as from our combined experience in social work and nursing of over 40 years in child protection work. These resources are designed to be applied in whatever context you practice, from primary through to specialist levels of support in voluntary or statutory agencies.

Chapter 1 provides the reader with up to date information about the new organisational arrangements within which child protection and safeguarding children practice is taking place following a period of significant legislative activity in children's welfare services.

Chapter 2 examines the crucial role of primary care and early intervention in preventing harm or neglect to children and young people. The rights of children and specific skills in helping them are emphasised.

Chapter 3 considers the causes, signs, symptoms and effects of child abuse. These are described, discussed and analysed to enable the reader to develop important assessment skills.

Chapter 4 explores how important multi-disciplinary and inter-professional care is in helping locate your practice within the appropriate network of statutory and voluntary resources to fulfil the aim of holistic support.

Chapter 5 provides readers with practical tools for assessment and risk management, the focus of which will help in complex work involving children and young people. Developmental and attachment theories are utilised particularly to aid in designing family support intervention.

Chapter 6 examines the process of protection by analysing elements of the legal and practice guidance available to practitioners to provide accessible information vital to effective intervention.

Chapter 7 focuses specifically on the needs, rights and responsibilities of young people as they struggle with the challenges involved in negotiating transitional points in their development. Staff are offered advice, guidance and practical skills to help safeguard the welfare of young people.

Chapter 8 describes and discusses culturally competent practice in order to distinguish the particular needs of a diverse multi-cultural and ethnically rich society. This forms part of a discussion on achieving socially inclusive anti-discriminatory practice.

Chapter 9 examines the subject of reviews and details how to end child protection work safely using knowledge and theory from a wide variety of sources underpinned by evidence-based practice.

Collaborative and co-operative, working together are too easily reduced to rhetorical devices as a kind of professional comfort blanket. In this text we deconstruct and analyse these concepts and maintain this critical focus centre stage to enable staff to embody the practice in meaningful ways directly in their work.

Partnership practice and service user evaluation is a growing area of interest in practice. This concept is developed and applied to the area of safeguarding children and young people throughout the book to illustrate the potential of an empowering, child-focused design and delivery of effective services that meets the needs and responds to the agenda of young people themselves.

A selected list of organisations that can offer resources that are directly or indirectly accessible to children and young people, as well as to parents and practitioners, has been included at the end of the book.

Terminology

The terminology in this book has been kept as accessible as possible within the confines of the editorial guidelines and the intended audience. It is necessary however to explain how certain terms have been used in order to at least offer the reader some context to understand their use.

We use the terms *child protection* and *safeguarding children and young people* synonymously throughout the text to reflect the current transitional phase of policy guidance and literature on this subject.

Culture is used in places where it is specifically defined but elsewhere it is used in the sense of the organisation of experience shared by members of a community including their standards for perceiving, predicting, judging and acting.

Black is used in the contemporary accepted sense of meaning that group of people who by virtue of their non-white skin colour are treated in a discriminatory way and who experience racism at the personal and institutional level every day of their lives.

Race as a term is declining in use due to its origins in meaningless anthropological classifications by early imperialists seeking to legitimise their exploitation of indigenous land and wealth. It is a social construction but one which is still found in statutes, policy material and in common parlance.

Ethnicity is subject to much definitional debate in the literature but for clarity and brevity the term is used throughout this text to mean the orientation it provides to individuals by delineating norms, values, interactional modalities, rituals, meanings and collective events.

Family is also a term around which there is some debate as it is both a descriptor and a socially prescribed term loaded with symbolism. In this book the term family is used to embrace the widest ethnic and cultural interpretation that includes same sex partnerships, single parent, step family, kinship groups, heterosexual partnerships and marriage, extended family groupings and friendship groups or community living arrangements.

Learning objectives

These overarching learning objectives have been designed to articulate new initiatives in building capacity and skills in the children and young people's workforce. They harmonise with inter-professional knowledge, skills and competencies required to enhance more effective collaborative work in child protection. A combination of practical skills development and evidence-based knowledge is enshrined throughout to maximise the ability of the community to safeguard children and young people:

- Contribute to the understanding and assessment of the needs and problems of children, adolescents and young people to ensure they are safeguarded and protected from harm.
- Communicate and engage with young people in a process of partnership practice that enables them to identify and articulate their needs and agendas.
- Demonstrate critical understanding of current policy and legal aspects of safeguarding children, young people, and their families.
- Demonstrate knowledge and awareness of the importance of socially inclusive and culturally competent practice.
- Communicate effectively in partnership with multi-disciplinary staff to collaborate and co-operate in delivering the care needs of children, young people and their families.
- Contribute to the effective planning, use of methods and models of intervention and reviews with children and young people and their carers or parents.
- Demonstrate knowledge of the requirements for evidence-based practice and the importance of effective evaluation in safeguarding children and young people

Learning profile

Below is a list of the learning objectives for each chapter outlined above. You can use it to evaluate your current understanding of safeguarding practice, and to decide how the guide can help you extend this. The profile is for general guidance or for use by trainers and educators. You might like to use it particularly in the early stages of your learning, or for further professional development in planning with peers and your employer. In training and professional education contexts the profile can be adapted for groupwork, teambuilding and inter-agency collaborative learning.

For each of the objectives listed below, tick the box on the scale that most closely corresponds to your present knowledge. You can use this to determine in how much detail you will need to study each chapter. At the end of the book you will find an identical list of objectives and the same scale – by completing this Learning Review you can gauge how much your learning has developed and on what areas you still need to work.

Chapter 1. A New Working Environment

I can:	Not at all	Partly	Very well
Describe how changing patterns of service delivery are influencing professional relationships.	○	○	○
Demonstrate understanding of the impact of new legislation, policy and guidance on safeguarding children and young people.	○	○	○
Describe the obstacles to, and ways to achieve effective multi-disciplinary work.	○	○	○
Understand the principles of integrated working.	○	○	○

Chapter 2. Primary Prevention and Early Intervention

I can:	Not at all	Partly	Very well
Acknowledge the rights of the child and young person across organisations whether survivor or offender.	○	○	○
Achieve an understanding of the family and its place in the community.	○	○	○
Understand the preventative framework required when working with children, young people and their families.	○	○	○
Reflect on individual skills and practices undertaken to promote children's physical, psychological and social well being.	○	○	○

Chapter 3. Children and Young People at Risk

I can:	Not at all	Partly	Very well
Understand modern explanations for child abuse.	○	○	○
Describe risk and resilience factors in children and young people.	○	○	○
Explore and understand the types and causes of abuse.	○	○	○
Identify the signs, symptoms and effects of abuse.	○	○	○

Chapter 4. Collaborative Care

I can:	Not at all	Partly	Very well
Comprehend the necessities of collaborative working across organisations.	○	○	○
Identify the barriers in the system against collaborative working and the approaches required for effective working together.	○	○	○
Review effective strategies for inclusive, integrated practice.	○	○	○
Reflect on the core skills required for working collaboratively across organisations including during inter-professional meetings.	○	○	○

Chapter 5. Assessment and Risk Management

I can:	Not at all	Partly	Very well
Develop familiarity with contemporary assessment tools for work with children and families.	○	○	○
Utilise developmental theories and models for assessing children and young people's welfare.	○	○	○
Recognise assessment as part of the continuum of care and therapeutic support necessary for safeguarding children and young people.	○	○	○
Understand the key issues and skills relevant to effective risk management in child protection work.	○	○	○

Chapter 6. The Process of Protection

I can:	Not at all	Partly	Very well
Understand the importance of clear planning and co-ordination for safeguarding children and young people.	○	○	○
Be clear about the stages of the child protection process and the legal framework supporting it.	○	○	○
Develop competence in using the provisions of the Children Act 1989 to safeguard children and young people.	○	○	○
Understand the ways in which the Human Rights Act 1998 can be used to support the welfare of children and young people.	○	○	○

Chapter 7. Supporting Young People's Transition

I can:	Not at all	Partly	Very well
Reflect upon the reason for and effects of risk taking behaviour in young people.	○	○	○
Understand the preparatory work required to support young people through transition from child to adult services.	○	○	○
Reflect on my changing role with the young person during and after transition.	○	○	○
Understand the communication issues and opportunities between practitioners and children and young people.	○	○	○

Chapter 8. Social Inclusion and Cultural Competence

I can:	Not at all	Partly	Very well
Describe what is meant by social inclusion and cultural competence.	○	○	○
Illustrate the importance of anti-discriminatory practice to safeguarding children and young people.	○	○	○
Explain what changes can be made to contemporary practice to meet the needs of a diverse society.	○	○	○
Describe the elements of socially inclusive safeguarding practice.	○	○	○

Chapter 9. Reviewing and Ending Safely

I can:	Not at all	Partly	Very well
Demonstrate the importance and purpose of a child care review.	○	○	○
Understand the significance of enabling the child to express their views.	○	○	○
Ensure that transfer of cases happens speedily with maximum inter-agency communication.	○	○	○
Describe the importance of reflective practice and supervision.	○	○	○

Using this guide

The exposition in the main body of the text will draw on a variety of sources, including government policy and best practice guidance, social, educational and health care theory and research findings. This will provide you with relevant information and knowledge to create the framework within which you can absorb, understand and then practically apply changes in your working context.

The activities you will be asked to complete are designed to help you recognise and understand aspects of practice which you might not previously have known about or considered, and will help you to develop self-awareness by inviting you to relate your experience to the issues being explored. The temptation is to skip the activities – try not to because they can be valuable in ways you might not anticipate at first sight. They are designed to give you the opportunity to bring your own experience into the learning process, but also your responses will build up into a resource which you can draw on in current practice contexts and future personal and professional development.

With this in mind, it is useful to keep a separate booklet in which to write your responses. Think of this as a form of **learning journal**, and record things such as experiences at work which seem to you to relate to specific activities you have completed from the workbook. This can provide useful practice material for future reference and revision on your own, in supervision or during consultation.

The activities are reproduced at the back of this book (pp.155–170) to enable you to photocopy them more easily. The circumstances permiting the photocopying of these activities as well as the Learning Profiles on pages 5–7 and pages 136–138, are explained on page 155.

Chapter 1

A New Working Environment

Learning Objectives

- Describe how changing patterns of service delivery are influencing professional relationships.
- Demonstrate understanding of the impact of legislation, policy and guidance for safeguarding children and young people.
- Describe the obstacles to, and ways to achieve effective multi-disciplinary work.
- Understand the principles of integrated working.

Structural and organisational changes to the way child protection services are delivered are the institutional response to improving the safeguarding of children and young people in the wake of the damning Laming inquiry into the death of Victoria Climbié (DoH, 2003) and The Bichard Report of the deaths of Holly Wells and Jessica Chapman (Home Office, 2003). *Every Child Matters: Change for Children* (2004) establishes the new framework for building services *around children* in which previously separate services must now work together in an integrated way.

Above all, these changes aim to provide professionals with consistent ways of communicating about children's welfare. In many ways communication is the most important because organisational change of itself cannot bring about shifts in entrenched attitudes, beliefs, customs and vocabulary. And despite repeated child abuse inquiries citing poor communication between agencies as one of the major reasons why children have not been properly protected, it remains difficult to get right. Reder et al. (1993, 2003) suggest that agencies need to put greater effort into understanding the *psychology of communication* in order to improve it. This means more than superficial and tokenistic exercises hosted by agency managers, but a fundamental re-appraisal of the knowledge, values and personal beliefs held by every member of staff engaged in work with children and young people.

You must consider this aspect of your work in safeguarding children as much a priority as learning new procedures and legislative guidance. Integrated working does not mean absence of disagreement – indeed the evidence suggests closer proximity with other agency staff *accentuates differences* between professionals. But this need not be a problem provided you work hard to appreciate each other's perspectives and not be so certain of your omnicompetence. Disagreement may actually be healthy and force staff to compromise or continue seeking a solution. At another level such differences between professionals may reflect the dynamics in the family situation which produce splits. Thinking about yourself as an *equal part of an integrated system*, rather than as an individual agency representative is a crucial re-conceptualisation to make.

Equally you should be wary of rushing too quickly to agreement and consider whether the multi-agency group are avoiding or denying some unanswered and complex issues because of the risk of exposing an argument. Self awareness is one of the keys to managing the stress and strain inherent in working together to safeguard children. This requires skilled and highly developed supervision skills from line managers and a willingness to expose your practice to scrutiny and to engage in reflective practice.

The Children Act 2004

The Children Act 2004 offers guidance on how to develop your individual practice to safeguard children and provides a legislative spine for the wider strategy for improving children's lives. This covers the universal services which every child accesses, and more targeted services for those with additional needs. The Act defines children and young people to mean those aged 0–19 but also includes those:

- Over 19 who are receiving services as care leavers under sections 23c to 24d of the Children Act 1989.
- Over 19 but under 25 with learning difficulties within the meaning of section 13 of the Learning and Skills Act 2000 and who are receiving services under that Act.

The overall aim is to encourage integrated planning, commissioning and delivery of services as well as improved multi-disciplinary working, removing duplication, increasing accountability and improving the coordination of individual and joint inspections in local authorities. The legislation is enabling rather than prescriptive and provides local authorities with a considerable amount of flexibility in the way they implement its provisions.

The Act set the seal on a series of developments for safeguarding children and young people's welfare that have radically changed the shape of provision and created a new organisational context for their protection:

Section 10 came into force in April 2005 and placed a **duty on local authorities and relevant partners to co-operate in order to improve the well-being of children in their area**. Well-being covers: physical and mental health; emotional well-being; protection from harm and neglect; education, training and recreation; the contribution made to society; and general well-being. These terms are not well defined and neither is the linkage between the separate elements. This could lead to very different perceptions from the variety of agency staff involved with the same child. The notion of co-operation includes working together to understand the needs of local children; agreeing the contribution each agency should make to meet those needs; effective sharing of information about individual children at a strategic level to support multi-agency working; and the commissioning and delivery of services.

To date schools and GP's have not been included in the specific list of 'relevant partners' in the Act mandated to co-operate and this has caused serious concern among child care organisations who fear the government's drive to increase the autonomy of schools will undermine the coherence and collaboration explicit in safeguarding policy. The National Youth Agency is also disappointed that youth work is relatively ignored in this legislation despite evidence of the effectiveness of youth workers in safeguarding young people. The government believes that other guidance such as that in *Every Child Matters and Refocusing Children's Services* (DfES 2003b, 2004) implicitly expects all agencies to co-operate in safeguarding children and young people.

Sections 11 and 28 introduced **a general duty of care on services to safeguard and promote the welfare of children.** This applies to the Children's Services Authority; schools; district council; strategic health authority; primary care trust; NHS or Foundation Trust; police authority; Probation

Board; Youth Offending Team; prison governor; and Connexions. The duty to co-operate is meant to lead to integrated services through: Children's Trusts; National Outcomes for Children and Young People; The Common Assessment Tool; Information Sharing Databases; and Safeguarding Children's Boards.

Safeguard means prevention of and protection from maltreatment. Promoting welfare means ensuring children and young people have opportunities to achieve physical and mental health; physical, emotional, intellectual, social and behavioural development. However current guidance on section 11 fails to establish a clear line of accountability between Children's Trusts and Safeguarding Children Boards or to make explicit how the two bodies relate to each other on child protection matters.

Section 12 provides for *the creation of a database to facilitate a new identification, referral and tracking system*. This was one of the key practical measures to emerge following the Laming Report and is an information system designed to enable all staff concerned about any child or young person to access a database to ascertain who else might be involved and contact them if necessary. However the aim of encouraging better inter-agency communication may well be at the cost of reducing the much valued confidentiality desired by young people in contact with sexual health, HIV and mental health services. There is no guarantee this information system will actually deliver better inter-agency communication and there is a real prospect of placing some young people at greater risk of harm if they are deterred from seeking help because of fears that their confidential details will be exposed.

The system should only contain the child's name, address, gender, date of birth, a unique identifying number, plus the name and contact details of any person with parental responsibility or day to day care of the child, education provider and primary care provider. A flag will indicate that a professional working with a child has a cause for concern. The nature of the concern would not be described on the system. This has attracted criticism because there are no published threshold criteria for *what constitutes reasons for concern*. The fear is that this is likely to lead to a variety of definitions from staff in different agencies and result in defensive practice whereby minor concerns are flagged to ensure legal cover causing unnecessary work. Guidance suggests that concerns need to be flagged when:

- **A practitioner feels that others need to know the important information that cannot appear on the database.**
- **That this information may affect the types of services made available to the child or young person.**
- **The practitioner has completed an initial assessment under the Common Assessment Framework and wants to discuss their findings.**

Security of this database has been questioned because of fears that a lack of staff training combined with the sheer numbers of staff able to use the system will invariably lead to a breach of security. Also users need to ensure compliance with the Data Protection Act 1998 and the Human Rights Act 1998 where client's rights will sometimes conflict with child protection procedures. Children and young people when consulted about this accept that information should be shared between agencies if it will help them gain access to the services they need. But they want to be consulted, know with whom it is being shared, and to be reassured that the information is accurate, will be used properly and kept safe.

The government has proposed that a lead professional should be designated to act upon information placed on the database, operate as a gatekeeper, decide whether information was merited and co-ordinate service responses. The recommendation is that this person should be someone from the agency with most day to day contact with the child. For most children this person will be their school teacher but teachers are resisting taking on this scale of responsibility.

Sections 13 to 16 provide for the establishment of local *Safeguarding Children Boards* which will replace the previous Area Child Protection Committees (ACPCs). Their responsibilities include:

- Developing local procedures.
- Auditing and evaluating how well local services work together.
- Putting in place objectives and performance indicators for child protection.
- Developing effective working relationships.
- Ensuring agreement on thresholds for intervention.
- Encouraging evidence-based practice.
- Undertaking part eight reviews when a child has died or been seriously harmed.
- Overseeing inter-agency training.
- Raising awareness within the community.

With Safeguarding Children Boards put on a statutory footing their expanded role will cover monitoring of practice, training and service development. The majority of this membership will be drawn from police, education, social services and health. Health can be particularly well represented from paediatrics, hospital trusts, the primary care trusts and Child and Adolescent Mental Health. The Probation Service, the Crown Prosecution Service, CAFCASS, the Magistrates' court, the NSPCC and other voluntary organisations are all likely to be represented (Murphy, 2004).

Sections 17 and 26 introduce *a new children and young people's plan (CYPP)* which from April 2006 is the strategic, overarching plan replacing the Behaviour Support Plan; Children's Services Plan; Early Years Development and Childcare Plan; Education Development Plan; ACPC Business Plan; Teenage Pregnancy Strategy and Youth Services Plan. The CYPP should set out the improvements that local authorities intend to make to meet the five outcomes for children and young people identified in *Every Child Matters* (2003):

- **Enjoying and achieving:** getting the most out of life and developing broad skills for adulthood; attending school and achieving national educational standards; achieving personal, social, development and enjoying recreation.
- **Staying safe:** being protected from harm and neglect and growing up able to look after themselves. Being safe from maltreatment, neglect, violence, sexual exploitation, bullying and discrimination. Protected from crime and anti-social behaviour. Learning and developing independent living skills.
- **Being healthy:** enjoying good physical health and mental health and living a healthy lifestyle. Being emotionally and sexually healthy and choosing not to take illegal drugs.
- **Making a positive contribution:** to the community and to society and not engaging in anti-social or offending behaviour. Making decisions and supporting community development and enjoying positive relationships. Choosing not to bully or discriminate, develop self confidence and manage challenges.
- **Economic wellbeing:** overcoming socio-economic disadvantages to achieve their full potential. Engage in further education or training and prepare for employment, family life and independent living. Access to decent homes, transport and sustainable incomes.

The Children's Services Authority (CSA) will lead the integrated planning and commissioning process by gathering the views of children and young people to identify their needs, circumstances and aspirations. The CSA will agree priorities, plan provision and identify resources from all partner agencies to contribute. Services can then be jointly commissioned, monitored and evaluated to assess their impact on the five outcomes.

Activity 1.1

Make space and time at your next team meeting or staff conference to include a discussion on the changes taking place within children's services. Try drawing up two lists: advantages and disadvantages and then build in future time to tackle the perceived disadvantages.

The proposals in the CYPP should be based around a needs assessment of the local child population, outlining a three year plan of action and specifying budget contributions from the relevant agencies. Workforce analysis should also be included in order to identify where skills shortages exist and to improve overall provision. Pooled budgets and resources will be extended using existing powers in the Health Act 1999, and the Local Government Act 2000 to ensure that funding required by the CYPP is targeted wherever it can impact on children's outcomes.

Section 20: provides for *joint inspections of children's services.* Ofsted will take the lead responsibility for creating a new framework for the inspection of children's services. Joint Area Reviews (JARs) conducted collaboratively between other commissions and inspectorates will evaluate regularly how well services, taken together, improve the well-being of children in a children's service authority area. Integrated performance assessment of local authority education and social care functions will contribute to the overall Comprehensive Performance Assessment (CPA) with JAR's connected to and using complementary processes designed to secure coherence and efficiency in monitoring and evaluating performance. Particular attention will be paid to children and young people vulnerable to poor outcomes:

- Children and young people who are looked after.
- Children and young people with learning difficulties or disabilities.

The Children's Commissioner

A Commissioner for Children in England was appointed in 2005 following the earlier examples of Northern Ireland and Wales which symbolises the importance of recognising the need for society to take seriously the children's rights agenda that should be an integral part of safeguarding practice. The Commissioner has a duty to promote awareness of the views and interests of children by:

- Encouraging persons exercising functions or engaged in activities affecting children, to take account of their views and interests.
- Advising the Secretary of State on the views and interests of children.
- Considering or researching complaints procedures related to children.
- Considering or researching any other matter relating to the interests of children with particular reference to the five outcomes for well-being.

Critics have pointed out that the commissioner is not independent enough and the terms of reference are not strong enough to properly represent children and challenge the government when necessary.

The European Network of Ombudspersons for Children have also criticised the way the Children's Commissioner for England cannot conduct an investigation into the case of an individual child. It is seen as a further weakness that the Commissioner has permission but no obligation, to have regard to the UN Convention on the Rights of the Child.

Re-focusing children's services around extended schools, together with new Safeguarding Children's Boards and new Directors of Children's services charged with a duty of care for corporate parenting by local authority lead councillors, altogether represent a significant re-configuration of existing structures and policies. The government policy is enshrined in *Every Child Matters: Change for Children* (2004) itself building on earlier proposals contained in *Every Child Matters* (2003).

Children's Trusts

The creation of most Children's Trusts is expected to be achieved by 2006 and all by no later than 2008, combining education and children's social services under one corporate director for children's services. By 2008 local authorities are expected to have completed the integration of these previously separate organisations. Evidence from surveys conducted by social care journals thus far suggests that each authority will adapt the process of change to local circumstances. There is no national blueprint so you may find yourself working in a 'virtual' trust where staff and services integrate when and where necessary with the focus on co-ordination of front-line teams with maximum flexibility. Or you might work in a physically integrated space occupied by a range of staff from various agencies.

Reflecting the children's rights agenda however there is an explicit expectation that children and young people will be *actively consulted* about service development. Inspectors in future will be seeking evidence of how your service is reaching out to, and engaging with, young people in order to establish genuine communication about their needs. Several children's charities and independent organisations have track records of representing children and young people and will be valuable partners in future developments in this important area of practice.

These are all part of the government's long-term aim to bring all commissioning for children's services together. Children's Trusts will be made up of the following key services:

- **Local education authorities** who provide educational welfare; youth services, special educational needs, educational psychology, child care and early years education and school improvement.
- **Children's social services** who provide assessment and provision for 'children in need', family support, fostering residential and adoption services, advocacy, child protection and support for care leavers.
- **Community and acute health services** include community paediatricians, drug action teams, teenage pregnancy co-ordinators, child and adolescent mental health services, health visiting and occupational therapy.
- **Youth offending teams** provide multi-disciplinary work with young people and their families to prevent offending.
- **Connexions** provide a multi-agency advice and guidance service for 13–19 year olds.
- **The police service** have expertise in domestic violence, child protection, truancy and tracking missing children

The need for Children's Trusts was prompted by the failings identified in the Laming inquiry into the death of Victoria Climbié. It is hoped that partnership working will be enhanced by the consolidation of previously separate responsibilities for children's services and to formalise joint work already successfully established in contexts such as Sure Start, the Youth Justice Board, the Children's Fund, Connexions and youth offending teams.

The Education Act 2002

The Education Act 2002 and guidance issued by the DfES in 2004 Five Year Strategy for Children and Learners, requires that every local authority in England should have some extended schools by 2006 and over 1,000 by 2008. The policy is intended to improve the outcomes for all children by enabling extended schools to provide integrated wrap-around services from 8am to 6pm including diverse activities involving local communities, playgroups, sports clubs, welfare, childcare, and health advice. Schools could offer co-located multi-disciplinary services in partnership with other agencies, children's trusts, businesses, other schools and voluntary agencies offering a range of resources, skills and support.

Many schools already provide additional services and activities centred on their premises such as counselling, attached social workers, after-school homework and sport. In addition a new role is being prescribed for school nurses by the Chief Nursing Officer whereby they will be much more actively involved in child protection, health promotion and parent support.

Section 175 sets out the legal duty on schools to safeguard and promote the welfare of children. The aim is that staff in the education service:

- **Provide a safe environment for children and young people to learn in education settings.**
- **Identify children and young people who are suffering or likely to suffer significant harm, and take appropriate action to make sure they are kept safe at home and at school.**
- **Contribute to effective partnership working between all those involved in providing services for children.**

However many child care organisations have pointed out that a significant number of children and young people are not engaged in schools and do not naturally regard them as a positive resource. Pupils excluded, receiving home tuition, attending specialist pupil referral units, or involved in regular truanting will need to be reached in other more creative ways if their needs are not to be neglected. They are arguably more in need than those already participating in school life and will be at higher risk of abuse and/or tempted into anti-social behaviour.

In 2004 there were 1,629 allegations of abuse against education staff in England, 66 per cent related to physical abuse, 15 per cent sexual abuse and 15 per cent to inappropriate behaviour. The Bichard report emphasises the importance of establishing safe employment strategies but points out that relying solely on the Sex Offenders Register and Criminal Records Bureau checks to identify paedophiles is dangerous. Most child abusers are unknown to the criminal justice system. Each school must ensure it has a designated senior member of staff and a school governor who has undertaken minimal child protection training. In addition every member of staff and all school governors must know the name and the role of the designated member of staff for child protection. School staff need to understand that they have an individual responsibility for referring child protection concerns and be alert to signs of abuse and how to respond to a pupil who may disclose abuse.

School child protection policy is expected to notify social services if a pupil on the child protection register is excluded or if there is an unexplained absence of a pupil on the register for more than two days duration (or one day following a weekend). Staff working with children with statements of special educational needs will need to be particularly sensitive to signs of abuse that could wrongly be attributed to disability or learning, emotional and behavioural difficulties or mental health problems.

The educational outcomes for looked after children are a reminder that safeguarding children is more than immediate protection from harm. In 2002 only 41 per cent of children leaving care obtained one or more GCSE's compared to 95 per cent of year 11 pupils. During the same year only 5 per cent of young people left care with five or more GCSE's compared to 50 per cent of all year 11 children (DOH 2003).

The National Service Framework for Children, Young People and Maternity Services 2004

The National Service Framework for Children, Young people and Maternity Services (NSF) is a 10 year programme intended to stimulate long-term and sustained improvement in children's health. It aims to ensure fair, high quality and integrated health and social care from pregnancy right through to adulthood. Overall, the NSF sets national standards for the first time for children's health and social care, which promote high quality, women and child-centred services and personalised care that meets the needs of parents, children and their families. The standards require services to:

- Give children, young people and their parents increased information, power and choice over the support and treatment they receive, and involve them in planning their care and services.

- Introduce a new child health promotion programme designed to promote the health and well-being of children from pre-birth to adulthood.

- Promote physical health, mental health and emotional well-being by encouraging children and their families to develop healthy lifestyles.

- Focus on early intervention, based on timely and comprehensive assessment of a child and their family's needs.

- Improve access to services for all children according to their needs, particularly by co-locating services and developing managed Local Children's Clinical Networks for children who are ill or injured.

- Tackle health inequalities, addressing the particular needs of communities, and children and their families who are likely to achieve poor outcomes.

- Promote and safeguard the welfare of children and ensure all staff are suitably trained and aware of action to take if they have concerns about a child's welfare.

- Ensure that pregnant women receive high quality care throughout their pregnancy, have a normal childbirth wherever possible, are involved in decisions about what is best for them and their babies, and have choices about how and where they give birth.

Standard five of the NSF states that **'all agencies work to prevent children suffering harm and to promote their welfare, provide them with the services they require to address their identified needs, and safeguard children who are being, or who are likely to be, harmed'.** The responsibility for contributing to this new multi-agency integrated framework rests with:

- Primary care trusts who are responsible for improving the health of their whole population.
- Strategic Health Authorities who are the performance managers.
- NHS Trusts who are required to designate a named doctor and nurse to take a professional lead on safeguarding children.
- Ambulance Trusts, NHS Direct and NHS walk-in centres who must have similar arrangements in place.
- Local Authorities who must ensure there is a designated professional for safeguarding children in social services, housing and education departments.

Safeguarding and promoting the welfare of children should be prioritised by all agencies, working in partnership to plan and provide co-ordinated and comprehensive services. Agency roles and responsibilities should be clarified to ensure that harmed children are identified and assessed as soon as possible by appropriately trained staff with suitable premises and equipment. Under the NSF an up to date profile of the local population must be compiled to facilitate needs assessment and to provide integrated services to meet that need.

Activity 1.2

Obtain a copy of your agency safeguarding children procedures and practice guidelines, or make sure you know where it is held and to whom you should refer in cases involving child protection.

Children's centres

It is envisaged that about 2,500 children's centres will be established by the year 2008 as part of the current government plan to provide universal access to affordable, flexible child care. They are another example of integrated strategic thinking where provision for under-fives, early education, full day care, parental outreach, family support, and health services can be offered. Children's centres are also expected to have a role in identifying and providing for children with special educational needs, provide a base for child minders, act as a service hub for other child care providers and offer management and workforce training.

These new centres are set to develop in different ways according to local need and local authority priorities. The concept includes full-scale centres in areas of high need and one-stop advice centres in areas where little more than information and signposting is required. Criticisms of the children's centre plan include the concern that they are replacing Sure Start programmes where there was an ethos of flexibility, and innovation built around parental expectations. Also, the role of the independent and voluntary sector seems to have been minimised in the strategic planning which does not bode well for partnership practice and integrated services.

This is reflected in Figure 1.1 which illustrates the new organisational structure for safeguarding children.

The Integrated Children's System

The government expects that professionals focus on the needs of individual children rather than the needs of the organisation. Therefore, structural change is less important than creating *a culture whereby staff learn to work in a more integrated and collaborative way.* This can be done by creating common assessment procedures, co-location of staff and more multidisciplinary teams. The aim is to reduce the number of separate assessments, thereby reducing time, potential confusion and duplication.

Studies of attempts of coordination have shown that you can integrate all of the services for some of the people, some for all of the people but not all of the services for all of the people (Leutz, 1999). A review concluded that joined-up government has to be seen as a long term, selective and cooperative project (Pollitt, 2001). Changing the way in which services are provided so that they become better integrated may require a more incremental approach in which the centre works in partnership with localities who learn by doing and the state learns by monitoring (Waldvogel, 1997).

The implementation of more integrated services for children will, therefore, need to demonstrate a clear purpose, be cooperative and flexible, focus on practice as well as structures and establish a culture of mutual learning that encourages the sharing and spread of knowledge with children and young people's active participation in this process. Developing the children's workforce is arguably the most important part of the integrated system agenda in which there are four main strategic challenges:

- Recruit more high quality staff into the children's workforce.
- Retain people in the workforce through better development and career progression.
- Strengthen inter-agency and multi-disciplinary working.
- Promote stronger management.

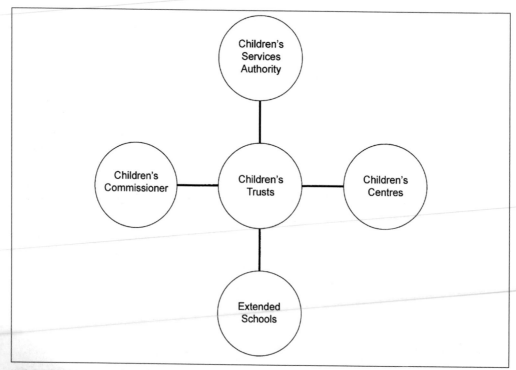

Figure 1.1   New organisational features for safeguarding children

The key aim is to create a single qualifications framework to enable transferable core and specialist units of knowledge so staff can more easily move jobs within the children's sector. Shardlow et al. (2003) in their work on inter-agency training and education discovered that few practitioner groups held any standards about their inter-agency practice. They suggest the following eight operational standards:

- Be clear about your own role and responsibilities in relation to those of others.
- Respect and, where necessary, challenge the views of other practitioners.
- Consult and communicate effectively with other practitioners.
- Evaluate collective judgements and conclusions about particular clients.
- Use and communicate relevant information within ethical boundaries of confidentiality.
- Collaborate with other practitioners.
- Review the progress of inter-agency collaboration at regular intervals.
- Record inter-agency communication and assessments.

The test of the success of all the above changes is whether children and young people will actually be better protected in a service that is demonstrably more cohesive and accountable. The evidence will be as much in the quantitative data used to measure such factors as in the qualitative experiences of children and young people and whether they *feel* safer and more listened to.

Activity 1.3

Consider ways in which your agency currently consults with children and young people about the service you provide. They may range from simple feedback forms available upon request or a more pro-active process of inviting comments from representative groups that are officially recorded in statistically meaningful ways. Together with a colleague think of ways consultation could be improved.

Commentary

Obtaining authentic testimony from children and young people is notoriously hard. They are conditioned to be compliant with adults and not complain. Evidence suggests that when sensitively consulted with they reveal more accurate information about their experiences and feelings. Making token gestures at consultation and partnership working is worse than nothing because it leads to poor data and complacency. The key is to understand the way children think and feel, especially when they are involved with child protection services where they will have mixed feelings and strong loyalties to parents. Feelings of guilt may well strong and dealt with by projecting anger and blame towards professionals, while also idealising staff who they feel have rescued them.

Inter-agency working

The much vaunted aim of joint working and closer collaboration has echoed throughout much of the past 30 years of child protection reports where children have been killed when problems in communication between agencies have occurred. In fact it appeared in the 1945 inquiry report into the death of Denis O'Neill – often cited as the first child killed while subject to child protection agency involvement. The Royal College of Paediatricians recently disclosed substantial numbers of trainee paediatricians expressing reluctance to become involved in child protection work because of legal action against some doctors by aggrieved parents (*The Guardian,* May 2005).

Recent guidance from the DfES suggests that teachers should receive more comprehensive child protection training that equips them to recognise and respond to child welfare concerns. But teachers' representatives say that teachers have enough work delivering the education curriculum and like paediatricians they are reluctant to refer concerns because of the reaction from parents. Thus the policy aspiration to foster closer collaborative working between agencies involved in safeguarding children and young people faces serious obstacles.

The principal reason given for failures in inter-agency co-operation is that one key individual within that system failed to fulfil their part of the process which resulted in a breakdown in the protective intervention. It is not the individual within the system but the structure of the system itself that is of key importance. That one individual within a system can be blamed for a child's injury denies the whole concept of collective inter-agency decision-making and responsibility. Agencies can fall into the convenient practice of finding a scapegoat reflecting a societal individualistic culture and the adversarial legal system: 'In Britain, when things go wrong, the system encourages a blaming of individual agencies and practitioners' (Murphy, 2000).

Staff working to safeguard children are united by a particular case or a particular inter-agency group but they are disunited by all the natural differences that exist between their professions and agencies. It is these crucial differences that are the blocks to good child protection work. Murphy (2004) indicates six key elements which hinder inter-agency collaboration:

- **Perspective and culture:** each agency can hold a perspective on child protection that is substantively different from that of other agencies. Differences in how we see the problem can lead to great differences in how we understand it, and how we then act towards it. Professionals define and explain child abuse in different and sometimes conflicting ways and adopt quite different stances about the way work should be undertaken.

- **Roles and responsibilities:** everyone working with children needs to know how their role fits with that of others. There is often confusion about the roles and responsibility of other disciplines. Although the different disciplines may acknowledge the same aim – that of protecting children – in order to do this they come together, maintaining their own separate roles within the wider whole. One of the advantages of inter-agency child protection training is that it allows an opportunity for the exploration and greater understanding of these different roles and responsibilities

- **Education and training:** Lord Laming's inquiry made several specific recommendations about the introduction of inter-agency elements in practitioner training and the improvement of ACPC training. The review of education and training that followed the Laming Inquiry discovered that few practitioner groups maintained standards of inter-agency working and that those standards that did exist were not held in common between practice groups.

- **Structure and power:** when practitioners undertake complex tasks they usually work within their own professional structure, with a clear understanding of how each part of that structure should behave and what will happen if it fails to do so. When those practitioners come to child protection work, they find that this is not the case. Although their agency instructs them to do the work, that work is controlled by the case conference and the distant ACPC/SCB. Within this system, practitioners are both instructed to cooperate within the inter-agency framework and to retain the right to independent action.

- **Language and communication:** information is power and sharing it symbolises some ceding of autonomy. Disagreements exist both as to the content of what is to be shared and about the actual value of talking together at all. What seems essential to communicate for one may seem a breach of confidentiality or peripheral to another. Although most agencies and professional bodies agree that confidentiality may be waived in the face of significant harm to a child, agreement on the threshold of significant harm is difficult, particularly where information is being shared between child and adult oriented agencies.

- **Anxiety:** is a constant companion of child protection work. It runs through from the highest managers, to practitioners and out to parents and children. This anxiety is part of the reason that child protection systems have become so proceduralised. It is not anxiety itself that is the problem, but how that anxiety is dealt with on an inter-agency and inter-professional basis. Failures at an organisational level to appropriately contain anxiety can permeate all aspects of the agency's work, as well as affecting its relations with the outside world and other agencies.

Inter-agency training

Following research into the extent to which inter-agency child protection training actually takes place seven operational standards for inter-agency training to safeguard children have been designed to facilitate better co-operation and inter-professional working so that practitioners (Salford, 2004):

- Understand their own professional or occupational roles and the roles of other relevant professional or occupational groups.

- Respect, critically evaluate and when necessary, challenge the views of other practitioners; also that they can and do learn from others and when appropriate disagree with, respect, or challenge the views of others.

- Know when and how to consult, communicate and share concerns, information and assessments about children with practitioners from other organisations, including when this is an investigation. Practitioners should understand the limits of their knowledge and responsibility and be clear about when to seek opinions from within their own organisations or from another organisation.

- Evaluate the judgements and conclusions made by themselves or other professionals about particular clients or cases.

- Use and communicate relevant information with due regard for the preservation of the client's confidentiality; they should know the ethical position of their own profession or occupation in relation to confidentiality issues, and act accordingly.

- Plan, undertake and evaluate collaborative work with practitioners from other agencies

- Participate regularly in reviews of the effectiveness and efficiency of inter-agency working through individual supervisory sessions, joint meetings and local evaluation and monitoring arrangements.

Activity 1.4

Make an effort to link up with a practitioner from another agency and meet to discuss the above and draw up an action plan to present to each other's teams to tackle the barriers to better collaboration.

If better communication is to happen it is essential that the practitioner or agency concerned:

- Behave in an assertive way by explaining the reasons behind a judgment or opinion to the rest of the inter-agency group.

- Never attempt to take over another agency's role or sphere of activity.

- Use the technique of predicting positive or negative outcomes for the proposed courses of action.

- Where possible, aim for compromise if not consensus. Where there is a sense that one side has forced a decision through, the probability of positive inter-agency co-operation being achieved around that decision is extremely low.

By being pro-active about potential problems and difficulties much goodwill can be generated and mis-conceptions dealt with before they occur during stressful situations. Acknowledging the powerful feelings aroused during child protection work in a safe environment away from the front line with a neutral facilitator can be very helpful in reducing all sorts of barriers to better communication. These training experiences are not add-on extras or self-indulgent experiential exercises. They are the real process by which learning takes place, practice improves and children and young people are better safeguarded.

Key Chapter Points

- Changes to the organisation and delivery of children and young people's safeguarding services are following legislative and policy guidance enshrined principally in The Children Act 2004, Every Child Matters 2004, and the Children and Young People's NSF 2004.

- Children's Trusts are set to become the core locus for the delivery of joined-up services for children and young people whereby staff from every agency will be expected to work collaboratively in multi-disciplinary teams or networks.

- The Education Act 2002 and Extended schools together with general duties to safeguard children and young people under the Children Act 2004 means that teachers and other education service staff will be expected to play a much bigger and more active role in child protection than previously.

- Staff working with children and young people need to learn about, understand and engage critically but positively with other agency staff who have different values, knowledge bases and skills in their perceptions of the needs of children and young people, who are or may be at risk of significant harm.

- Safeguarding children and young people effectively demands that staff make every effort to communicate with and overcome barriers to communication with all staff engaged in assessment or intervention to support families where vulnerable children and young people have been identified.

Chapter 2

Primary Prevention and Early Intervention

Learning Objectives

- Acknowledge the rights of the child and young person across organisations whether survivor or offender.
- Achieve an understanding of the family and its place in the community.
- Understand the preventative framework required when working with children, young people and their families.
- Reflect on individual skills and practices undertaken to promote children's physical, psychological and social well being.

This chapter seeks to explore and develop preventative work with children and families. Professionals have statutory authority in their work with carers and children. It is important that this mantle of power is wisely used to avoid oppression and abuse. Child care professionals are required to have critical awareness of government policy and need to strike a balance between their authority, methods of early intervention, and the rights of children and their families. Emphasis needs to be placed on the importance of knowledge and understanding of relevant frameworks, which enables work with families to be conducted in a way that builds on strengths. By promoting partnership you will be empowering parents and carers and thus protecting the child. Good practice endeavours to ensure that appropriate interventions are organised to support the child and in the majority of cases the family as well.

Children's rights to health and overall wellbeing were first raised as unique and different from adults within the Declaration of Geneva (1924) cited by Corby (2000) this highlighted the importance of several mainstays to supporting children and young people:

- welfare
- means necessary for normal development
- food and medicine
- relief in times of stress
- protection against exploitation
- protection against socialisation to serve others

UN Convention on the of Rights of the Child 1989

The convention indicates on a human rights basis what rights children ought to enjoy and what are the obligations of signatory states. Three principles underpin the Convention:

- All the rights under the convention must be available to all children without discrimination of any kind.
- The child's best interests must be a primary consideration in all actions concerning them.
- The child's views must be considered and taken into account in all matters affecting them.

In some ways the Convention goes beyond the principles contained in the Children Act 1989. First the Children Act established that courts have to regard the child's welfare as the paramount consideration. But under Article 3 of the Convention the child's welfare is a primary consideration across a wider range of settings where decisions about the child's welfare are made. So decisions about school exclusion or asylum hearings could be appealed under this article. Second, Article 19 seeks to protect children from all forms of maltreatment or neglect. This conflicts with current UK legislation permitting physical chastisement of children by smacking. Three other main principles enshrined in the UN Convention reinforce the philosophy of safeguarding children and young people:

- **Children have unique needs which set them apart from adults.**
- **The best environment for a child is within a protective and nurturing family.**
- **Governments and adults in general should be committed to acting in the best interest of the child.**

These rights are categorised into general rights to life, expression, information and privacy. More specifically the child should have protective rights against being exploited or abused. Civil rights are highlighted including the right to nationality and personal identity, along with the right to stay with the family. Alongside these is the acknowledgment that children should be in an environment which encourages development and offers a foundation for welfare (Moules and Ramsey, 1998). Special circumstance rights include children in war zones or other challenging situations were needs for safety have to be considered. The Children Act (1989) confirmed many of these ideas into British law and the Children Act (2004) continues the defence of children's rights including the right of protection from harm and to education, growth, health and well being.

The role of the family

To ensure that child care professionals are able to follow this through into their support for the family we need to start by defining what is meant by the term family. Each family is unique, however one popular definition suggests:

> The family is a social group characterised by common residence, economic co-operation and reproduction. It includes adults of both sexes, at least two of whom maintain, a socially approved sexual relationship, and one or more children, own or adopted, of the sexually co-habitant adults.

Murdock (1949) cited in Haralambos et al. (1991: 454)

The concern with this definition is that it does not relate to family circumstances in the 21st century, it is rather a media contrived idea that is narrowly focused.

The multiplicity of modern family structures is not acknowledged in mainstream discourse, no recognition is given to gay or lesbian couples with or without children, and alongside this there is a lack of realisation that cultural family groups may be cross-generational. The definition could also be seen as paternalistic in that a family is not seen to be complete unless there is a man present and therefore makes the assumption that lone parents, especially women, are not able to maintain a family.

The conventional nuclear family (General Household Survey, 2003) makes up only a small number of families in the UK today. The rise in divorce rates, the increased time children and young people have to stay at home and the number of individuals who prefer to live alone shatters the traditional definition. Families then can be said to be a collection of individuals who contribute to the collection of common characteristics and are accountable for each member of the group. This is greater than their responsibilities to others outside the group and this may or may not be linked to hereditary, adoption or marriage, (Fulcher and Scott, 1999). On the whole when exploring how to safeguard children we see the child or young person present in a variety of family groups usually with responsible adults acting as carers or parents.

Activity 2.1

Reflect upon the families that you work with; spend time highlighting the different styles of family structure. Analyse each structure exploring the strengths and weaknesses.
    Are there any common themes for the families?

The parenting children receive is a cornerstone for the development of their emotional, interpersonal and social well being .The quality of relationships they form with others, including their own children when they become parents, will be shaped by their care taking experiences.

(Reder and Lucey, 1995: 3)

Families may have common themes related to shared budgets and residency however it is the bond between members which truly reflect the spirit of family, and the desire to support care and love each other. Now that the details of what constitutes a family have been explored, it is necessary to discuss how to keep children safe in the wider arena of the community.

Safeguarding children in the community

Community can be defined as a group of individuals who have a common situation, which may be class, geographical location, or culture. The people within the community may share common activities such as work, politics or religion and they may undertake collective action to support each other. Finally the individuals may have a shared identity which could be related to culture, religion or sexuality (Fulcher and Scott, 1999). When examining the role of society and its responsibility to safeguard children and young people who are members of that society, issues arise around promoting a child-friendly community.

Poverty, poor housing and unemployment all make the situation more challenging both for the family but also for the local community, both with regard to health and social care. Secondly children and young people do not often have the opportunity to express their needs and perceptions, (NSPCC, 1996). Since the Black Report and the Health Divide cited in *Inequalities in Health*, by Townsend, Davidson and Whitehead (1988) it has been clear that families with less money and education endure more morbidity and higher mortality. This has been related to many concerns including general life style health and child protection risk factors:

- Lack of social integration.
- Cultural or religious tension.
- Attitudes to children and young people by the local community.

- Limited awareness of specific needs for children and young people.
- Imbalance of power.
- Poverty.
- Inconsistent pattern of employment.
- Limited access to services.
- Difficulty in obtaining information especially if English is not the first language.
- Inadequate transport services.
- Inadequate places for children to play.
- Inadequate places for young people to socialise.
- Inadequate educational provision.
- Inadequate leisure and sports facilities.
- High crime rates (especially violent crime).
- Lack of a forum to hear the child's or young person voice.
- Poor housing provision.
- Neglect and litter in the local environment.

While some of the factors affecting the wellbeing and safety of children require resources, other factors relate to public opinion of children and young people, with more emphasis now being placed on enabling children and young people to influence government policy. The creation of the role of commissioner for children is meant to progress this aspiration. This may see a change in the way children's opinions are viewed (Children Act, 2004). How society and child care workers in the community can keep children safe and prevent abusive situations occurring will be examined below.

Interventions

Both health and child care professionals see the need to highlight the different levels of prevention required, confirming that prevention of abuse is the ideal solution but if this is not achievable then early detection and intervention is the next best thing. Intervention is the practice of coming between or interacting with other humans, Trevithick (2005: 6) 'the purposeful actions we undertake as professionals in a given situation, based on knowledge and understanding we have acquired, the skills we have learned and the values we adopt'. The process of intervention therefore utilises skills and experiences to enhance professional practice.

While it is commonly acknowledged within health and social care settings that interventions are required, there are generally three levels of prevention to support the process: primary, secondary and tertiary. Smith (1999: 129) cites Fuller (1996) who describes the levels as 'primary prevention would prevent the emergence of a problem, secondary prevention would refer to working on a problem in its early stages and tertiary prevention would limit the damaging effects of a problem already established'.

Hardiker et al. (1991) also acknowledges a fourth level, arguing that Level 2 can be separated into mild and easily supported risk situations, and more serious situations which may require more intensive long-term support. Level 4 would be the work undertaken with the child when they are under the care of the local authority. All four levels will be defined and explored below.

Primary prevention

Primary prevention can be seen to work at the societal level and offers universal services acknowledging the general needs of the population and influencing individuals and families to make positive life style decisions. This can be published through media campaigns which encourage individuals to protect the wellbeing of themselves and their families. This includes advice on education, health and employment and may reduce the risk of the family requiring more specialist services, (Hardiker et al., 1991; Smith, 1999; Moules and Ramsay, 1998; Wilson and James, 2002).

Examples of primary prevention:
- self help groups
- family centres
- community project working with children and families
- good quality day care
- school based activities
- universal financial benefits for children (family allowance)
- Family Tax Credit
- NHS Direct
- good quality social housing
- easy access to health care
- easy access to local government and library services
- literacy and parenting classes
- strong links from the schools to the local community
- guidance services linked to schools, hospitals and health centres
- organised play or leisure activities (especially during school holidays)
- well resourced preschool nursery provision (rising 4 programmes)
- road safety programmes

Activity 2.2

Compile a list of the useful primary preventive resources you have in the community you work in. Highlight the most popular resources used.
  Compare these services and find the similarities that make the services popular.

Services that do not appear to have a secondary function, especially around surveillance, will be more popular as families may not feel comfortable if they believe details they submit may be used for more intrusive purposes (Reder and Duncan, 2003). With programmes such as Sure Start acknowledgement has been given to the issues surrounding poverty and the effect it has on the whole family.

Secondary prevention

Secondary prevention is normally understood as early detection and short-term intervention where children and families are offered more focused support from professionals involving home visiting, clinics and counselling. Browne suggests (2002: 61) 'such professional can be instructed to screen routinely all families who come into contact with the service they are providing and identify predictive characteristics'.

While predictive factors can be difficult when trying to confirm the potential for abuse, some tools have had more success than others. Post Natal Depression (PND) is a general depressive disorder, including symptoms of clinical depression. This can include tearfulness, insomnia, difficulties in eating, mood swings and general apathy. If the mother's resources and support are inadequate they may not have the emotional ability to be patient when the baby cries continually or will not sleep. What is agreed by all the professionals is that the earlier the detection of PND occurs, the more successful the outcome for both the mother and the child (Murray, 1997). One predictive tool developed which has been shown to be appropriate is the Edinburgh Postnatal Depression Scale (EPDS) where the mother grades herself on how she feels emotionally following the birth of her baby. The use of tools such as the EPDS seems a valid method of assessment which encourages awareness and helps to empower the mother rather than labelling her as mentally ill. However the assessment and subsequent score will only be successful if it leads to support, either by individual counselling or through group support.

Examples of secondary prevention:
- parenting helplines
- home visits
- child surveillance clinics
- drug and alcohol programmes
- anger management programmes
- parental support programmes in the home
- youth services
- parent support groups
- child development programmes
- community mothers' programmes
- parent training programmes
- preschool programmes
- duty services to provide rapid response
- family centres and support services
- counselling individually or in groups

For secondary preventive work to be successful it has to occur in a supportive environment rather than in isolation, so dealing with a child's behaviour difficulties would not be so successful if the family's circumstances were ignored. Macdonald (2002) comments that short-term solutions may often produce good results however for some families the intervention may require further input, especially were parents are learning new skills on how to support their child. As the child becomes older, different skills will need to be learnt, this is especially true for parents who have learning disabilities and who need long-term support and are more likely to have their child removed.

Tertiary prevention

Tertiary prevention is described as an increased level of input over a longer period of time when it is proven that abuse has occurred especially for more complex and long-term difficulties within the family. The idea is to stop the worst effect happening to the child and to avoid, if possible, placing the child in care. Individual work with the child and the family may still produce positive outcomes however the interventions require commitment on both the part of the child care professional, the child and the family to stay the course. To serve the best interests of the child in legal terms, local government and work practices should enable a model to function which focuses on the child and family while still being accountable for the long term outcomes.

Examples of tertiary prevention:
- behavioural family therapy
- play therapy
- cognitive behavioural therapy
- parent training
- group and individual work for parents
- direct work with children focusing on the abuse
- abuse specific programmes for child and non-offending parent
- brief focused casework
- short-term fostering
- respite care
- utilisation of statutory framework
- task centred casework
- family centres with focused work by centre workers
- family therapy
- family case conference
- family support groups
- refuges

Macdonald (2002) highlights the high attrition rates and the inconsistency of research undertaken within this area as a problem in determining how successful these supportive services are in the long run. Alongside this is the reality that the longer you leave a child in an abusive environment the more likelihood that the effect will be greater on their emotional wellbeing. Therefore there needs to be a clear time frame for when the intervention is deemed to have been unsuccessful and the child has to be removed from the environment.

Quaternary prevention

Quaternary prevention is the point at which the child is supported via the care system. The action taken is to lessen and turn round the damage that may occur from the parting of the child from their parents, which could lead to low self esteem, loss of personal identity, and disempowerment. These consequences need to be considered against the risk of leaving a child in a situation where positive change is failing. This approach highlights that 'the importance of maintaining links and collaborating effectively with parents and children is also indicated', (Hardiker et al. 1991: 350).

Examples of quaternary prevention:

- regular contact
- regular correspondence
- fostering
- respite care
- abuse specific programmes for child and parent/s
- direct work with children
- play therapy
- parent training

(Adapted from Hardiker et al., 1991)

The main aim of this level of intervention is to work with the child and their family, separately and together along with the inter-agency team. The only variation to other levels is that the focus of the work should keep to a minimum the trauma which could occur for the child when introduced to the care system, and to work with the family to reunite the child with their family (if possible) once safe enough functioning is restored into the family unit.

Activity 2.3

Find a copy of your job description and reflect upon which parts of your practice is undertaken at primary, secondary, tertiary and quaternary level. Where you are working at higher levels, consider ways you may be able to start preventive work earlier.

   If you are working at the primary preventive level, how can you utilise services and child care practitioners at the higher levels, to reduce the risk of progression for the children and families you work with?

Commentary

The focus of individual child care workers may be based around a particular level of intervention however by working together in an integrated way it should be possible to offer more opportunities for families to access services before crisis intervention is required. This could be in the guise of offering social service advice and guidance on benefit entitlements etc at a mum and toddler group arranged by a health visitor. Or youth workers from Connexions could attend a senior school assembly to showcase the services they offer. Family planning practitioners could be present at a baby clinic for example. The permutations are endless with the main aim being to provide the families with opportunities to ask for help *on their terms* before professional intrusion is a necessity.

   While exploring prevention and the different levels of intervention, differing beliefs surrounding types of intervention need to be acknowledged. While health workers on the whole wish to prevent or reduce the effect of illness or disability, a social care worker focuses on the needs of the individual and attempts to reduce the risk of family breakdown. Culturally sensitive approaches take on board the wishes and views of ethnic groups when planning services. Chapter 8 explores this further.

   A combination of these perspectives will ensure that the appropriate intervention for the child and their family will take on board the risk to the child's health, disability, family function and cultural diversity. Now a clear understanding of levels of preventive work has been explored, reflection is required on individual skills and practices undertaken to promote physical, psychological and the social well being of the child and their family.

Early intervention skills

Possessing:

- Formal knowledge or technical skills.
- Good interpersonal skills with children, young people and their families.
- The ability to manage your own work and time schedules.
- The ability to offer help and advice in a non-patronising, non-judgemental way.
- The ability to teach parents, children or junior colleagues.
- The ability to solve problems.
- The ability to utilise reflection both during interventions with families and after to continue to improve practice.
- The ability to make appropriate arrangements to care and support the family.
- The ability to establish clear priorities so that time is spent with the family.
- The ability to enable the family to feel empowered in partnership with child care practitioners.
- The ability to actively listen to the family and respond appropriately.
- The ability to remain calm and try to contain anxiety even when others are showing signs of distress.
- The ability to develop and draw upon a network of other child care professionals when necessary and reciprocate as requested.
- The ability to understand individual family's coping strategies.
- The ability to evaluate the child's progress, with the child and family where ever possible.
- The ability to anticipate difficulties and offer support.
- The ability to offer clear information and explanations when requested.
- The ability, when the situation requires, to use counselling skills (referring to a counsellor if more input is required).
- The ability to be an advocate for the child and interpret complex situations as necessary.
- The ability to manage professional boundaries.
- The ability to constructively challenge.
- The ability to acknowledge the need for supervision.

(Adapted from Procter et al. (1998), Trevithick (2005)

Activity 2.4

Drawing from the list above highlight which skills you use most often.
  Reflect upon areas that you need to work on to improve.
  Develop some strategies to ensure that you are able to use your skills to the best of your ability.

Commentary

All child care practitioners endeavour to place the child centrally both within their work and during times spent with colleagues discussing the children and young people under their care. Encouragement of the child and family to be empowered is a way to enhance their lives and reduce the risk of abuse. In the normal run of events planned play for a child sets up the child for grown-up gender responsibility. Play thus acts as a rehearsal of ways to behave in real life situations and within the construction of play the development of empowerment (Skidmore, 1994). However many children and families have learnt helplessness which causes them to become powerless.

This may be due to the view that they have of child care professionals especially if communication is a problem, or it could be related to their fear of the unknown and therefore reliance on others to take responsibility. Families can learn to become helpless because events have occurred outside their control such as unemployment or disability, or previous experience has shown them that any action they take will not rectify the situation (Hugman, 1991; Bentovim, 2002).

This notion of learned helplessness appears to be related more to people who express the view that negative things occur because they are incompetent rather than an external force caused the problem. The people who are more able to work through the helpless phase are ones who are aware that the event occurred, but it was outside their control. If we relate this to children who are at risk in the community, the child could believe they caused the abuse. If this is the case they need to be supported to work through their feelings in order to understand they are not to blame and can start to acknowledge that there are ways to become empowered.

Skidmore (1994) advices practitioners to help children and their families to find areas in their lives that they can control and encourage the child and family to make well informed decisions about the future. This has to be seen as a reciprocal relationship where the child care practitioner is able to let go of their power and the child, young person and their family have a wish to take up the power.

While persuasion may be a useful tool any attempt to force a person to take up this responsibility is more disempowering than the situation the individual may have originally been in. The way forward is to work in partnership with children and their families at all levels of prevention. The ability to work in partnership enables the family to decide their level of input for the parents and for the child themselves to acknowledge their rights. Not only that, the boundaries become more flexible enabling the child care worker to move in and out of the arena of care as the family requires.

To work closely and satisfactorily with families requires good communication skills, to work as an advocate means an ability to negotiate with other members of the inter-professional team, which again requires communication and co-operation. Finally to empower a child and their family means having the awareness to give information freely to ensure informed decision making. In short good interpersonal skills are the lubricant which enables the inter-agency team to function successfully for and on behalf of the child.

Key Chapter Points

- Children's rights and needs was explored focusing upon universal aims.

- An understanding of the family and its place in the community was placed in the context of common beliefs and values.

- Factors affecting the community's ability to safe guard children highlighted the need for adequate resources to support children's wellbeing.

- Exploration of the preventative framework required when working with children, young people and their families describe the four levels of prevention that coexist.

- Individual skills are required to promote well being and define the multifaceted role child care professional have to undertake.

Chapter 3

Children and Young People at Risk

Learning Objectives

- Understand modern explanations for child abuse.
- Describe risk and resilience factors in children and young people.
- Explore and understand the types and causes of abuse.
- Identify the signs, symptoms and effects of abuse.

In order to achieve a balance between family support and safeguarding individual children, professionals working with children and young people need to systematically consider the complex factors involved in the investigation, assessment and intervention in child abuse. This will enable you to offer a service that is both supportive of the child, young person and their families but also ensure the child and young person's needs remain the central focus. This includes the child and young person who may be vulnerable or who suffers abuse and also children who abuse or become young offenders.

Each child is unique and therefore blanket policies and procedures will not support every child, rather a focused approach is required that acknowledges the rights of the child to their own optimum growth and development. Children therefore need to feel safe in communicating with professionals about their worries, fears and aspirations. Practitioners need to draw upon a variety of resources which enable them to communicate about and explore abuse and the reasons behind abuse. In particular these resources should support child care practitioners' concerns about a child's physical, emotional, cognitive, social, and spiritual health in order to develop skills in a holistic understanding of their clients.

An increase in professional interest during the 20th century in the child and young person's well being has led to an examination of every aspect of a child's life. Foucault viewed this extensive interest in peoples lives as the 'clinical gaze', Smart (1992). While the ideas of emotional issues for children and young people had already emerged earlier in the century with the public health movement, it was perhaps in the early 1970s that these ideas came to the forefront so that professionals examined not only the physical and intellectual development of the child, but also their psychological well being.

Therefore producing a clear picture of what the 'normal' child developmental progression should be at every age, using quantifiable analysis, enabled the child or young person on the edge of normality to come under increasing scrutiny. Paradoxically the more defined the picture became the greater the increase of children, young people and families who were continuously monitored. The positive benefits of this meant that problems the child had could be resolved sooner through early intervention. The negative aspect is the over-standardisation of what was seen as 'good enough parenting'.

Reasons for abuse

There are three main theories of abuse (Corby, 2000; Wilson and James, 2002; Kay, 1999):

- **Psychological** theories focus on the instinctive and psychological qualities of the individuals who abuse. This approach argues that there is some innate characteristic within an individual, which places them at greater risk of abusing, their motivation being linked to biological or instinctive features of human behaviour. Child abuse may also be seen to be the result of deprived learning experiences of the carer which may lead to inadequate controlling techniques when trying to manage children's behaviour.

- **Social psychological** theories focus on the dynamics of interactions between the abuser, the child, and their immediate environment. This approach appears to be positioned between focusing on the individual and broader social factors. Therefore how the individual is able to relate to their immediate environment is seen as the cornerstone for these perspectives. While explanations are given to the relationships within the family, individuals are often seen in isolation separated from the wider social influences and stresses. Therefore, the political and wider social implication in the deterioration of neighbourhoods or social networks is often ignored (Corby, 2000; Wilson and James, 2002; Kay, 1999).

- **Sociological** theories emphasize social conditions and the political climate as the principal reason for the existence of child abuse and neglect. Feminist theorists highlight the strong connection between abuse which is overwhelmingly perpetrated by males against females and the patriarchal gender power disparity in society. Exploring the sociological perspective of child abuse is unsettling as it raises the issue of safeguarding children and young people to the level of society rather than the individual. This includes professional child care workers who when acknowledging this approach can feel that the daily intervention which they offer to families is often not enough to support family stress. This can lead to frustration as the worker cannot remove the family from poverty or the challenging social environment.

While all three main approaches have strengths and weaknesses each approach alone is unable to fully encompass the reasons for the occurrence of child abuse. Corby (2000) cites the *Ecological Framework* (Belsky, 1980) as a four level approach which recognises the different perspectives and how they interlink with each other. Thus in Figure 3.1 the *Ontogenic* (inner) circle explores what the individual parent or carer brings to the interaction with the child. The *Microsystem* in the next ring highlights how members of the family interact with each other. The *Exosystem* investigates how the family interacts within the immediate environment.

Finally the *Macrosystem* in the outer ring acknowledges the broader factors such as societies view on poverty and welfare and the impact this may have on the family. Appreciation of the way the different systems interact with each other enables the child care professional to offer support not just on the individual level for the child, and family, but can also incorporate the broader requirements the family and local community may have including the need for appropriate housing or medical care.

Risk factors

To embark on the exploration of how children and young people can be at risk a clear understanding is required of risk and the factors involved. The media are sometimes responsible for encouraging the belief that all children and young people are at risk as soon as they emerge from their home

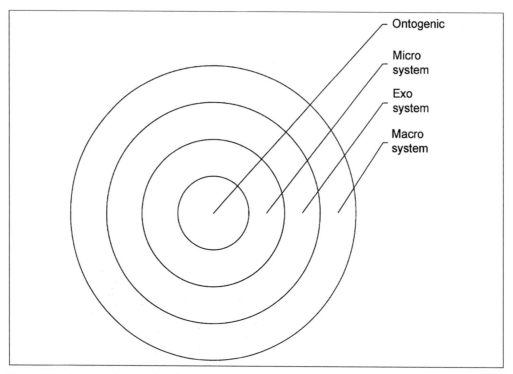

Figure 3.1   Ecological framework

environments. While it may be the case that many children are abused by strangers it should be acknowledged that children and young people are more vulnerable from abuse within their home environments by known relatives than in the streets (NSPCC, 2000). However, Rogers (2003) highlighted in her report for the National Family and Parenting Institute, when commentating on government policy surrounding children and young people at risk, that there are difficulties in defining a child at risk whether in the street or in their home environment.

The child at risk may present in a similar fashion to their peers both in relation to physical appearance and mental well being, and therefore may be difficult to assess. In reality, abuse usually occurs in an environment that the child is familiar with either within the home, school, or indeed their local community. Therefore all professionals regardless of their work setting need to be aware of the risk factors involved. The child or young person is at risk of abuse by family members or family friends. For some children and young people their peers may be the ones carrying out the abuse, the child or young person may be the abuser themselves, or they may place themselves in danger by willingly taking part in risk taking behaviour. It therefore becomes important to initially explore the risk factors which may produce circumstances within the family and local community that result in an inability to safeguard children and young people.

Specific risk factors:
- family violence or abuse
- drug or alcohol abuse (child or parent)
- changes in family structure

- parenting difficulties
- poor parenting history
- unwanted pregnancy (difficult birth)
- family conflict
- child living away from home
- child or parent disabilities (including learning disabilities)
- child or parental mental illness
- changes in family finances
- physical environment and accommodation
- availability of services
- attitude of local community towards child and family
- child or family isolation (either geographically or culturally)
- poverty
- age of parents (both ends of the spectrum can find childcare difficult)

(Adapted from Rogers, 2003 and Gregg, 1995)

These risk factors offer a broad outlook and only offer potential features, which may lead a child or young person to be at risk of abuse, carrying out abuse to others or indeed undertaking risk-taking behaviour. When reflecting on the ways to safeguard children and young people a consideration of the accumulative effects is required. It is also worth noting that while risk and protective factors and clear assessment frameworks offer guidance to the child care professional when supporting the child or young person, it is difficult to draw up a photo-fit picture of what the abuser may look like and their background.

Some families who have accumulated a number of factors may in consequence be unable to fully care and support their children. But it is also the case that for other families there appear to be no predisposing factors. Kay (1999: 15) comments:

> . . . there are no prescriptions for detecting that child abuse will take place in any particular family, but it may be that these factors can be taken in conjunction with other information to help identify the vulnerable families who may need support.

Activity 3.1

Spend 5 to 10 minutes reflecting on the community and families you work with, highlight both the general and the geographical specific factors which may lead to children, and young people within your area being at risk.

Would this list contain different risk factors if a colleague from a different agency or organisation undertook this activity?

Resilience factors

When exploring the record you have compiled it is worth remembering that this is a potential list. Some children and families may live through and survive emotional, physical, or financial trauma with their family life intact, while other families may not be able to endure relatively minor changes in family circumstances. This can be due to a number of resilience factors an individual or family may have. Werner (2000: 116) when exploring studies which have investigated the concept defines resilience 'as an end product or buffering process that does not eliminate risks and stress but that allows the individual to deal with them effectively'. She goes on to cite Garmezy et al. (1984) who surmise that there are three main mechanisms which enable these protective factors to occur:

- **Compensation** offers a framework where stress and protective factors counter balance each other and personal qualities and support can out weigh the stress.
- **Challenge** as a protective mechanism, highlights the strength that a moderate amount of stress can add to levels of competence.
- **Immunity** as the protective factors within the child or their environment moderates the impact of the stress on the child, and the child adapts to the changing environment with less trauma.

These models are not mutually exclusive rather they can work together or in sequence depending on the age and stage of the child's development. While there are a number of specific protective factors, these may vary over time depending on the child's age and resources available.

Protective factors
- low distress
- low emotionality
- sociability
- good self help skills
- average intelligence or above
- impulse control
- strongly motivated
- keen interests or hobbies
- positive self image
- self confident
- independent
- good communication skills
- good problem solving skills
- reflective learning style
- assertive
- positive set of values
- supportive peer group

(Adapted from Werner (2000) Corby (2000) Buchanan (2002)

Activity 3.2

Think of a child you have supported who appears to have coped well with the abuse they have survived. List the resilience factors they may have. Compare this with a child who was not able to cope so well.

Reflect upon how the knowledge that you now have may enable you to give appropriate early intervention in the future.

Commentary

Protective factors can also come from within the family including the skills of the mother or care giver to support and protect the child; this can include close family members and siblings who can also offer appropriate care to the child or young person. Within the home the encouragement of the child to develop independence including undertaking chores in the house can also support and protect the child. Werner (2000) also comments that having a strong faith or belief can give individuals a sense of stability even during personal, family or community crisis.

Finally the community itself can offer protective factors for children and young people, Bifulco and Moran (1998) comment that this can include having a supportive person in the neighbourhood, who maybe a relative, family friend, or peer, someone they can go to for support , and in the school environment from teachers and mentors. This support through the teenage years enables the individual to create a secure and safe environment for themselves.

Corby (2000) reminds professionals that while using predictive tools such as *The Framework for Assessment* (2000), which takes into account these risk and resilience factors, are of value when offering families services to prevent abuse, their success rate is not guaranteed. This becomes especially true when the abuse is sexual rather than physical or neglect. 'In summary these studies demonstrate that it is possible to predict between 65 and 80 per cent of known future abuse. On the debit side, however, it is fact that in this process at least 20 per cent of any sample is likely to be wrongly thought to be likely to abuse or neglect their children.' Conversely, a fifth to a third of all children being abused would still go undetected. Each child and young person is unique, therefore so are their families. When exploring risk and resilience characteristics you cannot always predict the families' responses even when appropriately assessed.

Concerns of children

Alongside the general risk factors, individual circumstances for the child and young person also need to be considered. In the green paper *Every Child Matters*, DfES, (2003) children and young people commented that they wished to be fit and well, feel protected and secure, enjoy pleasurable experiences, reach their potential ability, give something back to society and not to be poor. The Commission for Social Care Inspection (2004) asked children and young people about the concerns they had about feeling safe.

The report highlights the awareness of children and young people to the risk in communities and schools with regard to abduction, bullying, and muggings. The report continues that most children do feel safe, however some issues raised included worrying about being believed if they spoke out and concerned that the offender would not be appropriately punished. This clearly shows the need to acknowledge any issues raised by children and young people and follow through their concerns.

While abuse is a concern for every child and young person with regard to their individual experiences, O'Hagan (1993) and Bifulco and Moran (1998) argue that it is more complex as the effects of abuse are influenced by other factors. The type of association between the child and the abuser will have an impact. For example if the child sees the person everyday and consequently develops a constant fear of abuse may be more harmful than a child who sees their abuser infrequently. When the abuse is brutal, it could be more damaging than if the abuse is perceived as more restrained.

The child's age and stage of development has also to be taken into consideration, it may be argued that a young person who has already a clear picture of who they are may be less effected by abuse, no matter how severe, compared to a young child who is still discovering their own self worth and value. Finally, it could be argued that the duration of the abuse and how often the abuse occurs may also have a bearing on the long term outcome for the child or young person. However, each child and young person is unique and their level of resilience to the effects of abuse will also be individual to them.

Types of abuse

The types of abuse as defined by the DoH (1999) are divided into four categories, physical, emotional, sexual and neglect.

Physical abuse can be defined as physical injury to a child or young person presenting with an unconvincing story for the injury, and can been seen on a continuum from slight to severe and in a number of cases fatal. Bruises are the most generally seen symptom followed by fractures and head injuries (Kay, 1999).

Emotional abuse can be defined as the constant negative emotional behaviour of a carer to a child causing relentless and continual undesirable consequences on the child's emotional progression (Corby, 2000; Bifulco and Moran, 1998; O'Hagan, 1989). Emotional abuse by its very nature is implicated in every abuse the child endures as the words used by the abuser before, during or after the abuse are used to hurt, coerce or frighten the child or young person. It is important to recognise that emotional abuse may occur alone. Survivors of abuse often highlight the long term effects the emotional trauma has had upon them, while the wound from physical abuse can heal in a relatively

Shaking the child violently	Hitting, punching or beating the child
Throwing the child	Kicking
Throwing objects at the child	Scalding or burning
Grabbing, squeezing or crushing parts of the child's body	Fabricated or induced illness (FII) (Munchausen by proxy)
Scratching, pinching or twisting parts of the child body	Poisoning (this could include prescribed drugs)
Drowning	Smothering or suffocating the child
Breaking bones	Beating the child with an object
Biting	Stabbing or cutting

Figure 3.2   Common forms of physical abuse

Deprivation of emotional needs	Humiliation
Persistent negative attitude	Verbal abuse
Inappropriate development expectations	Inability to recognise child's individuality
Emotional unavailability and rejection	Telling the child, they are unloved
Frightening the child	Threatening the child
Inability to recognise child's psychological boundaries	Cognitive distortions and inconsistencies
Corrupting and exploiting the child	Ridiculing the child
Lack of warmth	Denying the child's achievements

Figure 3.3   Characteristics shown by abuser who emotionally abuses

short period of time, the emotional scars run deep, and may require intensive psychological therapy to aid recovery (Bifulco and Moran 1998).

While the above are the characteristics shown by the abuser, it can be more of a challenge to assess the effects that this abuse is having on the child.

Activity 3.3

Using the meanings of the behaviours in Figures 3.2 and 3.3 and give examples of how you think this is acted out in the family.

When exploring the behaviour of the abuser who is emotionally abusing a child or young person, spend time reflecting on how this may make the child feel.

It is worth bearing in mind that the fear which often accompanies emotional abuse can be just as traumatic as physical violence and not only affects a child psychologically but can delay their development and physical growth.

Remember that some of the effects on the child may not initially be linked to abuse; rather the child is seen as the individual who has problems, especially when linked to behavioural problems or disruptive difficulties.

Sexual abuse can be defined as forcing or enticing a child or young person to take part in sexual activities, whether or not the child is aware of what is happening (Corby, 2000). The activities may involve physical contact, including penetrative and non-penetrative acts. The majority of these assaults are perpetrated by known males but a significant minority by females.

While many individuals within society and indeed childcare professionals would like to believe that sexual abuse is a rare phenomenon (undertaken by sick or evil individuals), professionals need to be realistic about the number of children and young people who are abused, the NSPCC (2000) comment that sexual abuse is a significant form of abuse. The numbers of individuals who are survivors of sexual abuse are considerable. Some authors such as DeMause (1998) believe that there has been a historical global epidemic of sexual abuse, which is slowly improving.

However Corby (2000) comments that depending on the definition, the number of children and young people who claim to have been sexually abused varies in American studies from six to 62 per

Sexual assault	Child pornography, where sexual abuse is recorded
Sexual intercourse: vaginal or anal	Showing children pornographic material
Rape	Involving children in sexual activities
Masturbation of the child or of the adult by the child	Touching, fondling, or kissing the child in a sexual manner
Oral sex with the child or by the child	Indecent exposure
Child prostitution	Sexual activity with other children
Coerced sexual activity with animals or objects	Images of the abused child on the Internet

Figure 3.4   Sexual abuse

cent for females and three to 16 per cent for males. Corby also cites Mrazek et al. (1983) that 48 per cent of young college women reported being abused sometime in their childhood or teenage years. The statistics can however be seen as the tip of the iceberg, many authors and researchers confirm the difficulties in detecting and supporting the child and their non-offending carers following disclosures of sexual abuse (Bifulco and Moran, 1998; Corby, 2000; Kay, 1999; Wilson and James, 2002; Violence Against Children Study Group, 1999).

Children and young people, who have been affected by sexual abuse, have concerns that no one will believe them even if they are able to discuss what has occurred. Also they tend to have feelings of guilt because in some cases the perpetrator has groomed the child or young person over a number of years in a caring relationship and the sexual assault may not have been particularly painful. The child or young person may also have received gifts given as bribes in exchange for the abuse or financial rewards for the child and or their family, and finally the physical act itself may have felt pleasurable and in some cases the child or young person may reach an orgasm.

The child or young person who has been groomed and manipulated physically and emotionally may have been led to believe that this is normal loving family behaviour, until they discover that someone touching their body in an inappropriate way is abuse. Further guilt and emotional trauma may potentially occur following disclosure due to professionals, 'for example, it may be that not all abused children are traumatised by the sexual abuse in ways that continue to have an impact on their behaviour or to limit their outlook on life.' Bagley and King (1990: 220) cited by Trevithick (2005: 210) who continues '. . however, it is also possible that children can be traumatised by the manner in which professionals react and attempt to address their experiences of abuse'.

Activity 3.4

Abigail age 9 years old discloses to you that her daddy comes in to her bed at night and touches her. How would you ensure that she is given the opportunity to tell her story in a safe way, and how would you proceed following the event?

Commentary

Kay (1999) recommends an approach which is supportive of the child and offers them security. This includes listening without asking questions, controlling your emotions and not to become anxious.

Inadequate or inappropriate food	Inadequate or inappropriate clothes
Denying or failing to provide the child with adequate warmth and shelter	Not responding to the requirements of the child's developmental stage e.g. not toilet training the child
Failing to wash or bath the child	Failing to provide the child with clean clothing and a hygienic environment
Failing to supervise the child in potentially dangerous situations	Failing to seek medical attention when the child is ill or injured
Faltering growth (was Failure To Thrive FTT)	Failing to ensure attendance at school

Figure 3.5 Neglect

Also by reassuring the child that it's appropriate to tell their story but not promising to keep the information confidential. She continues that if the child appears to be in immediate danger reporting should occur straight away. Often children and young people are frightened to disclosure events because of the threats made by the sexual abuser. It may take an incident or sudden awareness due to knowledge gained about sex from school or peers that leads to the realisation that abuse is occurring.

Neglect can be defined as the continual inability to care for a child's needs, which may lead to grave harm of the child's physical condition or holistic progress. This delay in development should be in contrast to a child of a similar age and stage of development. Kay (1999) comments that neglect is a subjective category and professionals need to take care when citing neglect as occurring for the child. Some individuals may see handling of a child by a parent as neglectful but not so, by others. Inappropriate clothing for cold weather may be seen as neglectful. However, this may be due to lack of finances on the part of the parents, rather than a failure to protect due to inability to see the child's physical needs.

Activity 3.5

Melena is 4 months old and was born one month premature. Mum, who speaks very little English, has brought her to the health centre, as she is concerned that she is not really gaining any weight. She looks pale and withdrawn, and appears thin, and she is dressed in inadequate clothing. Mum says she is always hungry, and is consistently afflicted with minor illness.

How can support for mum be offered that ensures the child's and the entire family's needs are taken into account, including health promotion advice, interpretation, health and social assessment.

Commentary

It is important when exploring issues surrounding neglect to acknowledge that the inability to safeguard the welfare of children and young people is often not a conscious act. Rather some parents may be lost in a world of stress, isolation, depression or mental illness which inhibits their ability to care for themselves let alone their children. While other parents may not have the knowledge, cognitive ability or information to support their children, therefore while trying to offer the best for their children they may lack the capability to carry out appropriate child care. A significant number of parents may not have the personal or material resources to support their children.

Child's Development Needs	Parenting Capacity	Family and Environmental Factors
Health	Basic care	Family history and functioning
Education	Ensuring safety	Wider family
Emotional and behaviour development	Emotional warmth	Employment
Identity	Stimulation	Income
Family and Social relationships	Guidance and bounds	Family's social integration
Social presentation	Stability	Community resources
Self care skills		Housing

Figure 3.6 Framework for Assessment of Children in Need (2000)

This may mean that the whole family has a detrimental lifestyle, due to deprivation rather than conscious neglect. This leaves a small number of parents who may wilfully neglect their children, through lack of care or thoughtfulness; these parents place their own needs and desires above the needs of their children.

The child care professional, by using the *Framework for Assessment* (2000) has the opportunity to explore how the child is coping and how the family is dealing with their day to day lives. This will highlight if the child is in need and the resources which should be made available to meet this need. This should be in cooperation with the family and all the relevant agencies to ensure that a consistent and coordinated approach is obtained.

Commentary

The above framework can support Melena and her mother. It is important to explore the child's health needs to exclude any physiological reasons for the poor weight gain, however to ensure mum is part of the process the relevant interpreters need to be utilised. While in main cities this can be straight forward as services for speakers of different languages are relatively easy to access, this is often not the case in more rural areas, small towns or villages. Over the phone services can have some value, but it important not to use family and friends if possible as this can lead to confusion and mixed messages as they have an emotional link to the child and family involved.

The Violence Against Children Study Group (1999) comment that children who are black (they include all children who are non-white in this title) often receive an inadequate service compared to their white peers, due to the colour blind approach of many child care workers. This can be linked to language, culture and traditions, where stereotypes are employed as reality when assessing the family rather than taking on board the unique issues for each individual child and family.

The use of the inter-agency team will be paramount in Melena's situation, collaboration and cooperation will ensure that her health needs are explored, and following paediatric input, including investigations and health assessments, the team need to ensure that the support continues seamlessly into the community. While the health visitor will continue to monitor her weight and give mum advice on diet, nutrition and clothing, their social work colleagues will need to follow up with social support and financial advice. Housing colleagues may also be involved to explore issues related to the child's health and the accommodation available, while support groups (which may be religious or culturally based) or the education service may offer support in acquiring English language skills.

When reflecting on abuse of any kind including neglect, some types of abuse may seem obvious and easy to detect, others may not be so clear. The child may cover up injuries with clothing, or have plausible explanations for the cause of the injury. It is therefore necessary that individual judgements are made to decide whether the abuse needs further investigation. Another way to assess the situation is to observe for other changes in the child's behaviour, these are not necessarily indicators of abuse rather they are symptoms that a child or young person is upset or distressed (which may be due to abuse).

Signs and symptoms of child abuse

- stress related symptoms
- headaches
- stomach aches
- panic attacks
- eating disorders
- regression to wetting and soiling
- sexually explicit play
- clinging behaviour
- poor concentration
- self neglect
- mental illness (including psychosis and depression)
- nightmares
- disruptions in sleep patterns

The fear of abuse may lead young children to have frozen watchful awareness, where the child and young person watches everyone but remains perfectly still hoping not to be noticed. The child or young person may have sudden intrusive thoughts that lead to consequent actions including violence or aggression. The child may flinch for no apparent reason which may be a sign that the child is worried about being physically abused when someone moves close to them, while other children may wish to avoid talking about the events (Kay, 1999).

It is of paramount importance to ensure transparent and open lines of communication are pursued between the child or young person, their family and other professionals. Numerous inquires scrutinising gaps in services have cited poor communication and inadequate co-operation as the main component for unsafe practice leading to severe child injury or death, (DoH, 1999; Laming, 2003).

Children are predominately cared for in families and therefore it seems right that support should maintain the family environment where the child is 'safe'. However, if the family is assessed and found unsuitable for the child we have to ensure that intervention only supports the existing family unit while there is evidence for a positive outcome for the child. The child's well-being has to be seen as more important then any other factor in the family.

When assessing the abuse which may have occurred to children it is clear that this had to be placed in the context of what is inflicted on the child by the abuser rather than indicators that you may see that a child may have been abused. Some children are much more resilient to abuse than others, and where there are multiple risk factors this can sometimes be confusing. The rationale for this is that the signs and symptoms are often overlapping. It is also worth remembering that first impressions can be deceptive, both in terms of what is abusive, but also on how the situation is affecting the child. Integrated thinking about why child abuse occurs and how it may manifest gives us the opportunity to view the whole of the child's world, rather than the parent's or professional's perspective.

Key Chapter Points

- While a number of different explanations are given for the causes of abuse, an integrated approach acknowledges the multi-factorial nature of abuse.
- Risk factors can have an accumulative effect on the safety for the child or young person.
- Each child's resilience is dependent on the protective factors at their disposal.
- The majority of children are aware of the dangers they may face in their local community.
- The signs and effects of abuse can be difficult to detect and often overlap.
- The fear of abuse may lead children to change their behaviour.
- Children usually do not want to leave their parent rather they want the abuse to stop.

Chapter 4

Collaborative Care

Learning Objectives

- Comprehension of the necessities of collaborative working across organisations.
- Identification of the barriers in the system against collaborative working and the approaches required for effective working together.
- Review effective strategies for inclusive, integrated practice.
- Reflection on the core skills required for working collaboratively across organisations including during inter-professional meetings.

Over many years professionals have been encouraged by government legislation, national inquiries and local policies and procedures to work together to support, protect and safeguard children, young people and their families. This has recently been enforced with the Victoria Climbié inquiry (2003) led by Lord Laming, the publication of the green paper *Every Child Matters* (2003) and the subsequent Children Act (2004). However evidence suggests that the notion of working together appears to be a belief that is *valued but not always obtainable*. Therefore an exploration of the barriers to working together and the solutions to reducing or removing the barriers will offer resources to the individual professional concerned to achieve greater collaboration and cooperation. This will include exploring ways of networking and working successfully in a group. These are core skills for all staff and fundamental learning requirements for trainee and student social workers, nurses, youth workers and teachers and also any other individuals within statutory, voluntary or independent organisations, such as the police, private nurseries and schools, or professionals allied to health, who work to safeguard the well being of children, young people and their family.

Collaborative or partnership working are terms used frequently in the practice guidance and professional literature without a great deal of reflection about what the terms mean or how to realise them in practice. The Concise English Dictionary (11th edition, 2004) defines a professional as 'a person having impressive competence in a particular ability', this could relate to all individuals involved in the child's care from all specialities whether statutory, voluntary or independent. It could also be argued that it relates to parents and informal carers who may have extensive experience and knowledge about an individual child and their situation. Indeed it could be argued that children and young people are themselves the expert.

The dictionary continues by defining multidisciplinary (inter-agency or inter-professional is not defined) as 'involving several academic disciplines or professional specialisations', and continues that collaboration is 'working jointly on an activity or a project', however cooperation appears to be the most relevant word to use, defined as 'work together towards the same end' along with 'help someone or comply with their requests'.

These definitions bring together all the elements desired for pre-eminent practice within inter-agency working. This ensures that professionals are working together to agree a shared outcome for the child or young person and their family by having a common focus and by helping to support the child with the results they need for optimum growth and well being. Many inquiries have cited the lack of cooperation and communication across professionals and agencies as the reason why children have been harmed or killed by parents or carers. This was clearly highlighted in the seventies by the death of Maria Colwell and the subsequent public inquiry (Laming, 2003; Corby, 2000;Wilson and James, 2002; DHSS, 1974).

The main concern which came from this inquiry was to raise awareness of child abuse for professionals but also to improve inter-agency cooperation. This also led to the development of Area Review Committees, with senior professionals from all agencies working together to format guidelines across all agencies. The inquiry also heightened the recognition that case conferences were required to ensure all professionals were coordinating the services the child and their family received. Child care practitioners, especially around issues of child protection, were and still are consistently being blamed for poor cooperation.

Communication is important not only to support and develop relationships with families, but also to be able to work well with other professionals. Clients have concerns about the standard of communication they receive and it is the professional's responsibility to ensure it improves and acknowledge that the families personally need information throughout the child protection process.

Following the death in 1984 of Jasmine Beckford, another child involved with professional staff who was killed by her step-father, it was recommended that Area Review Committees became Area Child Protection Committee (now Local Safeguarding Children Boards) and that the Child Protection Register be more appropriately utilised to protect the child (Brent, 1985 cited in Kay, 1999, Wilson and James, 2002). Following on from these recommendations there was an upsurge in interventions and an increase in the number of children seen to be at risk and placed on the register. This illustrates the way government guidance produced in haste can impact on child protection practice.

Changing roles

The increase in numbers of children placed on the child protection register led to concerns by the public, fuelled by the media, of over enthusiasm by child care workers who were viewed as interfering and demolishing family life. Professionals were trying to adhere to new guidance and tread the fine line between appropriate intervention for the family and the need to protect the child. With so many professionals involved with child care issues including doctors, health visitors, social workers and the police it could be argued that events like the Cleveland Incident in 1987 were waiting to happen, where many children were removed from their homes following medical diagnosis of sexual abuse.

Analysis in this inquiry cited in Lyon and Cruz (1993) following the incident argued that not all the families required the intervention allotted to them. In some cases family behaviour viewed as worrying was perceived by the inquiry as on the fringes of normal behaviour. When viewed with the health professionals close scrutiny this appeared more severe than the reality. There is no doubt that many of the children involved were in need of support but the lines for engagement were confused. Fielding and Conroy (1994) believe this was due to lack of co-operation and communication between members of the multi-disciplinary team due to their differing and conflicting role in case outcomes.

In Cleveland, Butler-Sloss (1988) chairperson of the inquiry highlighted her concerned that health care professionals used a newly acquired Reflex Anal Dilatation Test for confirmation of sex abuse, and working alongside social workers, were seen to over-react to the increase in the incidence of child sexual abuse. In total 121 children and young people were removed from their parents and taken to a place of safety under wardship proceedings over a five month period.

All suspected cases of sexual abuse need investigating, however care needs to be taken to corroborate medical diagnosis, and in decisions about the need to remove children from their homes. The confusion in Cleveland occurred due to the different approaches the agencies undertook:

> *Social Services Department acted swiftly and authoritatively to secure place of safety orders on all diagnosed cases and the police and the police surgeons, who would usually have been closely involved in gathering evidence for possible prosecution, disassociated themselves completely from what was happening.*
>
> Corby (2000: 43)

While individuals were demonised because of the immediate outcome for the children and young people and their removal from their homes to a place of safety, it needs to be remembered that professionals believed they were protecting children. It was subsequently established that a significant number of the children and young people had indeed endured abuse. However due to the lack of inter-agency co-operation and collaboration there appeared to be inconsistent care of the child's and families needs. The government acknowledged this problem with the recommendations from this inquiry being incorporated into the 1988 *Working Together* documentation, which gave guidance about improving arrangements for inter-agency co-operation. This included the involvement of parents in case conferences wherever possible and the requirements that all professionals are involved in case conference decisions.

The Children Act (1989) reinforced the need to balance power between the family and the agencies working to support the child or young person within the family. Since the introduction of the Act changes have occurred within social services to ensure parents are involved in the decision-making processes even when the child is removed from home. However, as *Protecting Children, A Guide For Social Workers* (DoH, 1988: 9) remarks 'where there is a conflict of interests between parents and the child, the child's interest must be given first consideration'. So decisions that may be good for the family can only be taken if they are also beneficial to the child. However this ideal was shattered with the inquiry into the alleged ritual sexual abuse in the Orkneys.

One of the main issues besides the traumatic treatment of the children during the removal and interview process in this case was not that professionals did not work together, rather that parents were not seen as part of the team (especially the non-offending carer). Munro (2002) sees this approach from the public perspective as child care professionals, especially social workers having too much power to intervene in family life. On the other hand it could also be seen as a way to ensure that children are protected from unnecessary suffering.

Leathard (1994) believes that in present practice most practitioners working within teams which would include child care professionals who are safeguarding children and young people, feel that working collaboratively is a good approach and that this is a more frequent occurrence than in the past (Wilson and James, 2002). The value of this approach is especially true when resources are shared and the needs of the child and family dominate the discussion. Morris (2000) agrees in her report for the Joseph Rowntree Foundation and National Children's Bureau on barriers to change in the public care of children. She adds that social services, education and health services have been endeavouring to work jointly at local, strategic and national level.

In actuality practitioners who are often arranged in specialist groups tend to retreat behind professional lines every time important developments to inter-professional working are made. Morris also comments that there are often gaps between intention and practice. When concerns or issues arise that bring professionals into conflict especially around serious injuries to children or child murder, rather than working the issues out as an inter-professional team, individual professional groups often withdraw behind their professional identities and roles and are unable or unwilling to offer inter-agency support (Leathard, 1994; Corby, 2000).

This retreat frequently occurs when a crisis or issue arises – instead of individuals supporting each other across agencies and sharing experiences for caring for the child and family. Professionals tend to seek support from colleagues from the same professional background believing there would be greater understanding of the stress involved (Wilson and James, 2002; Morris, 2000). It is crucial therefore to explore and learn to overcome the barriers which prevent practitioners working together to safeguard children and young people.

Overcoming barriers to co-operation

Kearney et al. (2000) suggest that although the interfaces between organisations will change all the time (usually through structural change) the difficulties of working across the interface remain. These blocks to communication and action are not totally removable – they exist as an inevitable by-product of the boundaries between different agencies and practitioner groups. Their presence is therefore inevitable. However, the power of these blocks to affect practice is variable and if recognised and overcome by the practitioner as well as the agency, their power is significantly reduced. Rather than deal with each block individually, there are a number of steps that we can take collectively to reduce their power:

- **Willingness to ask the 'naive' question**
  If the combating of ignorance about other agencies is the way to reduce blocks to inter-agency working, one of the most useful techniques the practitioner can utilise is the insistence on asking the naive question. This technique makes a virtue out of asking for an explanation when you don't understand, you half-understand, or when you do understand but know that others do not.

- **Understanding and valuing the other perspective**
  It is important to accumulate the minimum amount of relevant knowledge that enables us to see the world from others' point of view. Once the knowledge about the other practitioner's role and perspective has been gained, good inter-agency work demands that this be put into practice. This means that the differences that individual practitioners bring must be included in the inter-agency process rather than ignored, bulldozed or pushed into a corner. Some strong element of compromise is suggested here rather than seeking a 'right' or 'superior' answer.

- **The dissemination of knowledge**
  The practitioner needs to be able to communicate in an intelligible fashion, the essential characteristics of their own agency, role and language to the other practitioners in the system. This closely reflects the ability to communicate. It implies the ability to share the information that you possess in such a way that colleagues appreciate what you are saying, what it means in terms of your agency, and its pertinence with regard to the particular case.

- **The ability to practise in an inclusive, inter-agency fashion**
  This is the key to overcoming structural blocks to inter-agency work. Although poor practice can seldom be laid at the door of the individual practitioner, positive inter-agency practice can be stimulated by individuals taking control over the inter-agency element of their own practice. The ability to practise in an inter-agency, inclusive way involves a change of thinking and the development of the 'inter-agency mind-set' (Reder and Duncan, 2003). This change moves from the position of 'I' and 'you' or 'they' to 'we' and 'us'. 'How can my agency sort out this child protection problem?' changes to 'how can we help the inter-agency team begin to address this problem?' It involves beginning to think about the work in a multi-agency fashion, to develop a cognitive map that is truly inter-agency in its focus.

Dealing with conflict

When the structural blocks to communication have been overcome and the human issues around working together have been dealt with, the potential for conflict between practitioners or agencies is still present. But it is likely that this conflict is concerned with professional differences of opinion or judgment, or a reflection of differences of interest within the family. It is important, according to Furniss (1991) that these differences are not minimised or ignored, but recognised, confronted and addressed, so that the issues in question can be resolved.

Poor communication between agencies occurs with:

- Power struggles between key professionals involved in the child's care.
- Traditional thinking with regard to services offered by specific agencies.
- Lack of motivation by individuals to invest time in working together.
- Different values and beliefs surrounding professional practice.
- Different and competing priorities in regard to outcomes for the child and family.
- Geographical location of offices or services.
- Differences in terminology used across agencies.
- Different philosophical frameworks used across agencies.
- Lack of priority given to joint service planning.
- Agencies different interpretation of their safeguarding responsibilities.
- Concerns about client confidentially across agencies.
- Lack of knowledge and stereotyping of practitioners from other agencies.
- Inaccessibility of staff across agencies due to different work practices.
- Budget restraints on local services for children and young people.
- Individual practitioners not able to incorporate inter-agency policies into their practice.
- Different threshold criteria across agencies for making decisions, especially around significant harm.
- Inconsistent levels of commitment of various professionals, especially following case conference.
- Diverse pre-qualifying educational curriculum input on safeguarding children and young people.

Activity 4.1

Make a list of all the individuals you work with, remember, to note not just the practitioners you work with on a daily or weekly basis, but those professionals who you may contact infrequently.

Within your practice area reflect upon the barriers that you can see in working effectively with all your colleagues both within your agency and across agencies.

Commentary

Some barriers can be geographical related to distance between child care practitioners. This is especially a problem in rural areas were distance may be considerable. Other barriers could relate to traditional thinking and the inability to see beyond the aims and objectives of the organisation. It is more important to focus on the child or young person rather than the needs of the organisation, however sometimes the systems put in place make this difficult for individual practitioners to move away from. All professions have unique philosophies which are derived from their educational experiences working practices and surrounding environment. This can lead to clashes across agencies when differing priorities arise.

Health, social care and education may not have a common understanding of care management. This means careful negotiation is required to ensure a balance of power is maintained to support the child and their family. An example of this may be the way that issues of confidentiality are dealt with both within a particular agency and also across agencies. While it is clear to all child care practitioners that confidentiality cannot be guaranteed, endeavouring to gain consent to share information with appropriate parties is tricky. It is important to sensitively ensure that the child or young person is aware that some information cannot be kept a secret, but will be dealt with in the appropriate manner and will not be a matter for public knowledge. However this is more complex around issues concerning health especially sexual health and any interventions required, where the equilibrium between patient confidentially has to be balanced with the health needs of the individual or others (Moules and Ramsay, 1998; DoH, 2003). If the child or young person is seen as Fraser competent (Gillick), this will also impinge on the outcome of sharing undisclosed information given in confidence (Wilson and James, 2002).

The process becomes more difficult and complex when sharing information across organisations due to concerns about breaches of confidentiality. The DDA (1998) clearly highlights the rights of individuals to confidentiality and privacy however it also clearly states that this does not restrict information for individuals, children, young people or adults who are seen as vulnerable. The DoH (2003: 43) guidance on giving information and advice when dealing with potential child abuse situations supports this view, 'sharing information amongst practitioners working with children and families is essential. In many cases it is the only when information from a range of sources is put together that a child can be seen to be in need or at risk of harm'.

Hendrick (2005: 264) highlights the current government view of the situation 'clause 8 of the Children Bill (Act) provides for the removal of all legal barriers that prevents professionals agencies from sharing information about children, without prior consent of the child's parents or the child her/himself'. This is where the confusion often lies in that it would be difficult to maintain a transparent and trusting relationship with the child and their family if this route alone was taken. However in some situations when the child may be at risk there could be some justification.

However Hendrick (2005) goes on to comment that this should be carefully employed especially when dealing with young offenders, as this has ramifications for fairness and justice to be seen to have been carried out. Ideal practice would be to share information, with all interested parties including the child, young person and their families after gaining consent, thus ensuring cooperation from all members of the family including the parents.

Interagency collaborative practice

While barriers exist it is important to acknowledge it is not a choice to decide whether or not to work across agencies rather, it is important to reduce the barriers in a way that supports the child, young person and all the professionals involved. This is now a statutory requirement whereby a framework has to be developed for cooperation across all agencies to support the wellbeing of children in your local area (Children Act 2004). This approach acknowledges the role of individuals from voluntary organisations, informal carers, private and statutory organisations and the need to combine and integrate services where appropriate. The family role within this cannot be underestimated. Carers often have to relay information between agencies and can still feel taken for granted by the caring professionals (Leathard, 1994; Lindon, 2003).

Multi-professional working

Advantages	Disadvantages
Collective sharing responsibility	Time consuming consultation
More efficient use of staffs (enabling development of specialists)	Increase in admin and communication cost
Effective service provision (overall service planning)	Conflicting and different leadership styles, values and language
Satisfying working environment (more relevant and supportive services)	Reduced independences and autonomy of practitioners
Better risk management, auditing of services and research	Difficult for professionals to make individual decisions
Ease of access for children and families	Inequalities in status
Development of new ideas, roles and ways of working	Minimises the importance of professional differences
Opportunity for shared supervision	Risk of professional collusion
Enhancement of professional skills	Separate educational backgrounds
Avoidance of isolation for practitioners	Blurring roles
Efficient sharing of education and resources	
Promotes professional openness	

Figure 4.1   Multi-professional working

Activity 4.2

Reflect upon the team you work in; highlight all the commonalities you share, including qualifications, knowledge and experience. Now highlight all the differences you may have.

Compare and contrast how these similarities and differences bring strengths and weakness to the group.

Commentary

The practice of multi-professional working can lead to efficient sharing of information and enhanced communication across agencies and helps to ensure greater cohesiveness and effectiveness within and across organisations to safeguard the child or young person and their family. The Children Act guidance for the NHS (1989) suggested that a plan for each child or young person was the best way forward which may encourage multi-agency working as the:

> ... *plan devised jointly by the agencies concerned in a child's welfare which co-ordinates the services they provide. Its aim is to ensure that the support offered meets all the child's needs, so far as practicable, and that duplication and rivalry are avoided. The plan should specify goals to be achieved, resources and services to be provided, the allocation of responsibilities, and arrangements for monitoring and review.*

(DoH, 1989: 54)

This is further supported in the *Framework for Assessment* (2000) where practitioners assess and plan services together alongside the Looked After Children (LAC) materials, all of which are focused on the needs of the child and young person and the requirement to overcome inter-agency barriers (Horwath 2001). Different agency managers should not be able to work alone, rather a pooling of resources should occur to ensure a common approach to child care services.

Unfortunately the Children Act Report (DfES, 2003: 27) discovered that:

> **30% of updated child protection plans were unsatisfactory. However all agencies accepted that they have a fundamental responsibility to ensure that children are safeguarded, and in most cases this was backed up with a firm commitment by senior managers to ensure that their agencies did so.**

In addition the DoH (2003) developed a straightforward document *What to do if You Are Worried a Child is Being Abused*, which progresses the child care practitioner through a number of flow charts highlighting the appropriate approach to take if you suspect abuse is occurring and how to work alongside other professionals. Initially *Every Child Matters* (2003) saw the way forward to safeguarding children to be based around the development of inter-professional teams within Children's Trusts which would be made up of health, education and social services. This has now become more flexible depending on the local organisational set up already in place, with the emphasis on improved inter-agency and inter-professional working and sharing of resources, rather than inter-professional teams which would geographically and organisationally come together.

The focus is therefore placed equally on the individual practitioner and the inter-agency team suggesting how to manage the initial suspicion through to the case conferences. The initial assessment allows the child care worker to investigate whether any action is required, and sometimes there are clear signs of harm or neglect. It is much more difficult to decide on whether the child is suffering from emotional or physical neglect and although there are procedures laid down to follow, these can be clouded by the experiences of the care worker. However if the child care worker believes there is cause for concern and time available which will not jeopardise the child's safety, then a case conference should be called (Kay, 1999; Lindon, 2004).

The main arena which highlights the requirement for inter-professional collaboration is during the case conference and subsequent reviews or for children with medical needs or disabilities. The purpose of the multi-professional meeting (multi-disciplinary) being to 'assess new cases and review on going casework' and involve all front line staff, (Corby, 2000). *Messages from Research*, DoH (1995) highlighted the problem in trying to achieve this, with meetings often being called at short notice meaning some professionals are unable to attend due to fixed working practises and other commitments.

This has been especially true for teachers, and GPs, who have the lowest attendance, however this is being redressed by the Royal College Of General Practitioners who have developed with the DoH a framework to encourage GPs with a special interest in child protection to gain more knowledge and support (DoH, 2003). The case conference should enable every person, professional, voluntary or family to make a contribution to the discussion on the way forward for the child. All children have the right to be included, however in reality this occurs only if they seem able to understand and cope with the proceedings.

The notion of a case conference is positive, people who care about the child come together for the child and this offers an opportunity for practitioners to share information (Wilson and James, 2002). However it is also an area of potential conflict between the family and care workers. Lindon (2004) comments that child and parental participation in case conferences is necessary for the family to have full access, however some professionals do not like parents attending conferences because they inhibit the overall discussion in the conference, both of professionals and the child if they are present, (Munro, 2002).

Wilson and James (2002), alongside Ferguson and O'Reilly (2001) believe some professionals in trying to pacify parents do not put the needs of the child first. Also parental anger may be aimed at professionals contributing unpleasant observations during the meeting. If information was shared with parents before the meeting then the tension may not be so great, as unexpected and unflattering evidence may not prepare the parents for open discussion.

Another area of conflict relates to the working partnership of the different professionals within the meeting. Their general aim may be the same, protecting the child's rights but the specific objectives are sometimes different. This conflict seems most obvious with the roles of the police who have to investigate the evidence for the opportunity to prosecute the perpetrator of abuse, and the social workers who need to support the child. The conference enables new information to be shared with the whole team however this may cause a change in the balance between the roles of members of the conference.

This can lead to professional rivalry as the social worker and police child protection officers try to enforce their viewpoint. Munro (2002: 156) comments that group reasoning can also lead to Groupthink in case conferences leading to conformity which is also unsafe for the child. This can occur in three forms:

- **Overestimation** of the group due to the history of success with previous cases the conference team may then take undue risk of outcomes for the child.
- **Closed-mindedness** can occur when reports from professionals not present and professional stereotyping of colleagues may lead to disregarding of evidence they present.

- **Pressures towards conformity** ensures that any outspoken criticism of the majority decision is censored until everyone is seen to comply with the general consensus of the group. A way forward for this is to have clear ground rules for behaviour of the whole group and also individual strategies to ensure that the child remains the focus.

Improving communication

Individual strategies

- Collect evidence from all colleagues who work with the child and family.
- Follow up your intuition with a non-judgemental investigation of the facts.
- Prepare your report in plenty of time and be familiar with the contents.
- Be honest with the parents before the conference.
- Ensure information is kept in chronological order and as complete as possible.
- Actively listen to other members of the group and keep an open mind.
- Be assertive and clear when presenting your information.
- Be prepared to constructively challenge other members.
- Be prepared to receive constructive criticism.
- Remember to use professional judgement rather than emotive statements.
- Give a sensitive but honest opinion of the child's situation.
- Do not let the potential for intimidation hold back your profession opinion.
- Show respect and value everyone's view regardless of whether they match your own.
- Do not be afraid to bring conflict to the group.
- Remember the child/ren should be the main focus.
- Maintain an anti-discriminatory focus.
- Professional judgement should override any personal dislike.
- Ensure you receive regular supervision to discuss issues raised at conference.

Activity 4.3

Reflect upon the last case conference or inter-professional meeting you attended, drawing on the points highlighted above. Give an honest critique of your performance. What did you do well and what were you unhappy about?

Write yourself some notes and points specifically for how you may change your practice at these meetings in the future.

Commentary

While it is important to reflect upon personal behaviour during a case conference, review or inter-professional meeting, this alone cannot offer the support the child may require both in the short or longer term. Rather it is the behaviour of all members of the group and their ability to critically reflect on the evidence presented to them that will determine the outcome for the child. This is clearly lead by the chairperson and while an indecisive or judgemental chairperson may impair the process, Munro (2002) makes the point that a good leader will encourage group discussion, valuing all participates present regardless of their role or status, and refrain from commenting on their personal opinion until later in the meeting. A further element to add could be a member prepared to play devil's advocate, who would have the role and sanction of the group to challenge any assumptions or complacency that may arise. However the whole group also has to take responsibility for the outcome of the meeting.

Group strategies

- Children who wish to attend need to be prepared.
- Parents who wish to attend need to be prepared.
- Remember that the child/ren remain the focus of discussion.
- Everyone needs to introduce themselves fully and the reason for their presence.
- Professional stereotypes must not override professional judgement.
- Members should be encouraged to share all information including that which is confidential.
- The group should avoid unrealistic optimism.
- Members should endeavour to remain objective rather than emotive.
- Balance must be given to ensure that valuing cultural diversity does not lead to tolerance of abuse.
- While support of the family should be central the needs of the child should be paramount.
- Reports from practitioners not present should receive equal weighting to those presented in person.
- All members should feel able to fully take part in the discussion.
- All members present should be prepared to vote on the outcome regardless of their specialty or background.
- All members should use straightforward language rather than professional terminology or jargon.
- If the child is not present to offer their wishes and feelings this needs to be acknowledged when decisions about their future are made.

Following case conferences there may be no further action or a key worker may be appointed – usually a social worker, but if the child is deemed to be at risk they are placed on the child protection register and an action plan is put into effect by the key worker. This is positive as it gives the child a way forward either with or without their parents. If the child remains at home then a variety of services may be offered, including home support worker, nursery nurse placement and parenting classes, also links to Sure Start and Connexions but much will depend on the resources and budget available.

The child remains on the register until a decision to deregister has been taken at case conference which are used at regular intervals to review the progress. Once a child has been registered it is up to the parents to prove that either there was no case to answer or that they have improved their parenting skills sufficiently to do without professional intervention. While safeguards are extremely important in protecting the child's rights, if the system wants to put the child first then when parents show a need to be heard and fully informed this should be considered as evidence by the care workers that parents as part of the inter-agency group are trying to put their children's needs first.

Professional skills can also be improved when practitioners share experiences thus reducing the risk of isolation. Alongside this, efficient sharing of education and resources which focus not on the agencies needs, but rather on the learning and supervision needs of the child care practitioner, is helpful. This can be further supported with professional truthfulness, combining materials both about particular children and their families and also information about up to date knowledge, research and evidence based practice leading to enhanced communication. This may facilitate the collaboration both within organisations which have a variety of professionals working with children, and across organisations with professionals having a common theme of focusing on the child. Care needs to be taken to ensure that professionals who have fixed workloads are given enough time to rearrange their workload to attend case conference and other meetings.

Working together

Strategic ways

- **Joint education:** both during prequalification education and for continuous professional development.
- **Joint policy:** for undertaking assessments, reviews or interviews.
- **Joint research:** both locally on specific issues for local population and nationally for general trends.
- **Joint commissioning:** both of universal service for all children and families and specific services for children in need or at risk.
- **Joint agreements:** for agendas with consensus of opinion for aims and objectives.
- **Joint protocols:** across agencies for sharing of information.
- **Joint sharing:** of early concerns to encourage preventive or early intervention.

The DfES (2002) confirmed that improvements were taking place in child protection and that SSD and other statutory partners especially in health and education were enhancing their collaborative working. However there are practical ways to further enhance the way practitioners work together. Morris (2000: 34) gives a specific example from the London Borough of Ealing where the council set up a Members Task Force:

> . . . it's a healthy working group, chaired by the Chair of Social Services but with representatives from all political parties. They've put aside their differences to work actively to achieve a working group which simply devotes its time to children's issues and nothing else.

Practical ways

- Start informal breakfast clubs, coffee mornings or lunch time meetings so that colleagues across different agencies in your local community get to know individual people rather than the stereotype.
- If time is a scarce resource, set up a website or chat room to catch up with how people are doing in all the agencies in your geographical locality (remember to set clear guide lines about confidentiality).

- Undertake joint visits to achieve a shared perspective on the situation for the family.
- When supporting families offer joint interventions.
- Share information about case loads regularly not just when required.
- Develop a users group of children young people and families who can offer comments and opinion on changes to local policies and practices.
- Ensure that an up to date community profile and needs assessment includes all services and resources available (evaluating their effectiveness).

(Adapted from Riley (1997) BASW (2003))

Activity 4.4

List the resources in your area which enable you to get together with colleagues across organisations; this should include formal meetings and informal opportunities.

Keep a diary and make a commitment to contact a variety of colleagues in other organisations on a regular basis.

Commentary

To work closely and satisfactorily with families requires good communication skills. To work as an advocate for the child means an ability to negotiate with other members of a team and across agencies which again requires fluent communication. Finally, to empower a child and their family means having the awareness to give information freely to ensure informed consent. In short, good communication is the oil which lubricates and enables the inter-professional team to function smoothly and successfully for the child. Child protection policy and procedures regarding children who are still living at home, the method of referring, use of case conferences and action plans emphasize the need to incorporate the child's needs and rights as well as parental involvement.

The terms partnership and collaboration are often used interchangeably to describe both the form of organisation and method of working. Harrison et al (2003) remind us that partnership working is pointless unless it can be demonstrated to have influenced policy and practice. White and Grove (2000) suggest that four elements must exist within a partnership in order for it to function:

- **Respect** without respect between partners there can be no prospect of achieving partnership.
- **Reciprocity** requires that partners contribute what they can on an equal basis without power resting in one agency.
- **Realism** requires a realistic appraisal of the challenges, tasks and resources.
- **Risk-taking** requires that agencies court failure even if this goes against instinctive practice.

For a child to voice their fear of abuse takes great courage, and while most professionals appear to take into account the problems the child has, welfare decisions are often made *for* the child rather than *with* the child. Professionals need as a team to put the child's rights first when making decisions, and it is only when this occurs that child care professionals can believe protection policies do protect the child and their rights. Great strides have been made, but with the knowledge known about gaps in services leaving children at risk, child care professionals need to continuously monitor procedures and their policy of inter-agency working to ensure that decisions are made in the child's best interest.

Key Chapter Points

- The background and history of inter-agency working showed how gaps in communication and collaboration led to avoidable child deaths.

- Barriers against collaborative working revealed the traditional practices and fixed view that professionals often have of each other.

- The necessities of collaborative working across organisations highlighted the enhancement of the child's support.

- Core skills required for working collaboratively across organisations explored individual and group practice and focused on case conferences, joint working and commissioning.

- Individual strategies for case conference or inter-professional group meeting highlighted the need to be clear and assertive in your professional beliefs.

- Group strategies for case conference or inter-professional group meetings discussed the requirement to be supportive of other professionals while keeping the child centre-stage.

- Strategic ways of working together provide solutions to ensure a seamless service across agencies and organisations.

- Practical ways of working together offers the practitioner some realistic solutions to break down the barriers to inter-professional co-operation.

Chapter 5

Assessment and Risk Management

Learning Objectives

- Develop familiarity with contemporary assessment tools for work with children and families.
- Utilise developmental theories and models for assessing children and young people's welfare.
- Recognise assessment as part of the continuum of care and therapeutic support necessary for safeguarding children and young people.
- Understand the key issues and skills relevant to effective risk management in child protection work.

There are many situations where harm – significant or otherwise – or the potential for harm to happen to a child or young person can arise. Assessing these situations is difficult for many reasons and more so where it is the *potential for harm* to occur that worries staff working with children and young people. Prediction in risk assessment is notoriously difficult and there is no reliable method or model that can offer practitioners any degree of certainty. A parent with a drug problem living in insecure accommodation may appear at first sight to be potentially neglectful but upon further assessment found to be providing 'good enough' care. With proper support and efforts to obtain appropriate housing they can be helped to cope and meet their child's needs more fully.

On the other hand an apparently successful middle class couple in their own home, each in secure employment might have an acrimonious separation in which their children are emotionally damaged witnessing domestic violence and being used as psychological weapons by each parent. Neither wants to engage in support services or mediation and resort to hostile communication via expensive lawyers. The children's behaviour at school and mental health deteriorate to the extent where one takes a serious overdose of paracetemol, and triggers investigation which reveals child protection concerns.

The important point to consider is that the very act of assessment can create additional stress and anxiety in both you and the family you are working with. There is pressure and expectation that can begin to distort the helping relationship and produce negative consequences on parent's and children's behaviour. The art of assessment is to suspend judgement and stereotyping and to analyse evidence from a variety of sources. There are skills to assessment and there are assessment tools, checklists and priority matrixes but they should be used to *support, rather than drive* your relationship with clients.

Research shows that a partnership approach to this aspect of safeguarding children is more likely to result in a positive outcome and increased safety, rather than a bureaucratic, rule-driven process which families experience as alienating and punitive. This adds further stress which pressurises parents who are already feeling vulnerable and resentful (Wattam, 1999; Jack, 2004).

Prevalence of abuse

Solid data about the prevalence of abuse is difficult to obtain but a reliable indication is that about 750,000 children will have been abused by the time they reach 18 years of age, with 400,000 having been sexually abused (Cawson et al., 2000). This NSPCC research suggests that about 30 per cent of girls have been sexually abused and about 15 per cent of boys. For the year to 2002 there were 70,000 section 47 child abuse enquiries with 50 per cent of those (34,800) also the subject of a child protection conference. 25,700 children were placed on child protection registers, continuing the downward trend of recent years.

These official statistics seem to imply that child abuse is decreasing which is not the case, rather they illustrate the shorter time spent on registers consistent with the reported increase in de-registrations. Thus we see that during the year up to 2002 there were 27,800 registrations. The problem with child abuse is the often hidden nature and secrecy surrounding it combined with societal ambiguity about state intervention in family life.

The common core of skills and knowledge for the children's workforce

This is an attempt to enhance integrated practice in safeguarding children. The main elements of the common core skills are (DfES, 2005a):

- **Effective communication and engagement** includes establishing rapport and respectful, trusting relationships; understand non-verbal communication and cultural variations in communication; active listening in a calm, open and non-threatening manner; summarising situations to check understanding and consent; outline possible courses of action and consequences; ensuring people feel valued; understand limits of confidentiality and relevant legislation; report and record information.

- **Child and young person development** includes observing behaviour in context; understand child development process; evaluate circumstances in a holistic way and distinguish fact from opinion; know when to refer on for further support; demonstrate empathy and understanding; support the child/young person to reach their own decisions; take account of different parenting styles; distinguish between organic disability and poor parenting producing delayed development; understand attachment patterns and the inter-relationship between developmental characteristics and being clear about your role and how to reflect on practice to improve it.

- **Safeguarding and promoting the welfare of the child** includes ability to recognise overt and subtle signs that children/young people have been harmed; involve parents and carers in promoting welfare and recognising risk factors; develop self-awareness and the impact of child abuse; build confidence in challenging oneself and others; understand legislation, guidance and other agency roles; share information in the context of confidentiality; appreciate boundaries of your knowledge and responsibility. Respond appropriately to conflict, anger and violence and understand that assumptions, values and prejudice prevent equal opportunity.

- **Supporting transitions** includes recognising changes in attitudes and behaviour; empathise and reassure to help child/young person reach a positive outcome; consider issues of identity and the effects of peer pressure; understand key areas such as divorce, bereavement, puberty and family break-ups, primary to secondary school, unemployment, leaving home; knowledge of local resources and how to access information.

- **Multi-agency working** includes effective communication by listening and ensuring you are being listened to; work in a team and forge sustaining relationships; share experience through formal and informal exchanges; develop skills to ensure continuity for child or young person; know when and to whom to report incidents or unexpected behaviour changes; understand how to ensure another agency responds while maintaining a focus on the child/young person's best interests.

- **Sharing information** includes making good use of available information such as a common assessment; assess the relevance and status of different information and where gaps exist; use clear unambiguous language; respect the skills and expertise of others while creating a trusting environment and seeking consent; engage with children or young people and their families to communicate and gain information; share confidential information without consent where a child is at risk; avoid repetitive questions and assessment interviews; appreciate the effect of cultural and religious beliefs without stereotyping; understand the Fraser principles governing young people's consent; distinguish between permissive information sharing and statutory information sharing and their implications.

The Common Assessment Framework 2005

Government guidance indicates that this instrument should be the main and sometimes only assessment instrument to be used at the first sign of emerging vulnerability, and to act as a marker for referral to another agency or specialist service. Assessments have hitherto been used to make decisions about whether or not a child meets the threshold criteria to trigger delivery of a service. The concept of the Common Assessment Framework (CAF) is that this should lead to a common approach to needs assessment, as an initial assessment for use by statutory or voluntary sector staff in education, early years, health, police, youth justice or social work. It is intended that this will reduce the number of assessments experienced by children and foster improved information sharing and thus help dissolve professional boundaries.

The framework is expected to contribute to the wider culture change across the children and young people's workforce by offering (DfES, 2005b):

- General guidance on its use.
- A common procedure for assessment.
- A methodology based on the Framework for the Assessment of Children in Need and Their Families (DoH, 2000).
- A focus on child development and communication skills with children, carers and parents.
- Gaining consent.
- How to record findings and identify an appropriate response.
- How to share information when a child moves between local authority areas.
- An explanation of the roles and responsibilities of different agencies and practitioners.

The framework needs to be familiar to staff in adult services and agencies that may not directly focus on the needs of children and young people, but indirectly contribute to achieving the five outcomes (see Chapter 1) for well-being. The assessment should be completed with the full knowledge, consent and involvement of children, young people and their parents. It should be child-centred, ensure equality of opportunity, be solution and action focused, and be an ongoing process rather than a one-off event.

The assessment must be centred on the child or young person and the whole spectrum of their potential needs, rather than the policy focus and statutory obligations of particular services. Outcomes from the CAF should be the identification of the broader needs of vulnerable children without additional support. Earlier intervention is expected from practitioners looking outside their usual work area for additional support. This should reduce the number of assessments undergone by children and families by improving the quality of referrals between agencies.

The Process of the Common Assessment Framework

- **Preparation:** you talk to the child or young person and their parent. Discuss the issues and what you can do to help. You talk to anyone else you need to who are already involved. If you decide a common assessment would be useful you seek the agreement of the child/young person and their parent as appropriate

- **Discussion:** you talk to the child/young person, family and complete the assessment with them. Make use of additional information from other sources to avoid repeated questions. Add to or update any existing common assessments. At the end of the discussion seek to understand better the child and family's strengths, needs and what can be done to help. Agree actions that your service and the family can deliver. You agree with the family any actions that require others to deliver and record this on the form.

- **Service delivery:** you deliver on your actions. Make referrals or broker access to other services using the common assessment to demonstrate evidence of need. Keep an eye on progress. Where the child or family needs services from a range of agencies a lead professional must be identified to co-ordinate.

The elements of the Common Assessment Framework

Development of baby, child or young person

- **General health:** includes health conditions or impairments which significantly affect everyday life functioning.

- **Physical development:** includes means of mobility, and level of physical or sexual maturity or delayed development.

- **Speech, language and communications development:** includes the ability to communicate effectively, confidently, and appropriately with others.

- **Emotional and social development:** includes the emotional and social response the baby, child or young person gives to parents, carers and others outside the family.

- **Behavioural development:** includes lifestyle and capacity for self-control.

- **Identity:** includes the growing sense of self as a separate and valued person, self-esteem, self-image and social presentation.

- **Family and social relationships:** includes the ability to empathise and build stable and affectionate relationships with others, including family, peers and the wider community.

- **Self-care skills and independence:** includes the acquisition of practical, emotional and communication competencies to increase independence.
- **Understanding, reasoning and problem-solving:** includes the ability to understand and organise information, reason and solve problems.
- **Participation in learning, education and employment:** includes the degree to which the child or young person has access to and is engaged in education and/or work based training and, if they are is not participating, the reasons for this.
- **Progress and achievement in learning:** includes the child or young person's educational achievements and progress, including in relation to their peers.
- **Aspirations:** includes the ambitions of the child or young person, whether their aspirations are realistic and they are able to plan how to meet them. Note there may be barriers to their achievement because of other responsibilities at home.

Parents and carers

- **Basic care, ensuring safety and protection:** includes the extent to which the baby, child or young person's physical needs are not met and they are protected from harm, danger and self-harm.
- **Emotional warmth and stability:** includes the provision of emotional warmth in a stable family environment, giving the baby, child or young person a sense of being valued.
- **Guidance, boundaries and stimulation:** includes enabling the child or young person to regulate their own emotions and behaviour while promoting the child or young person's learning and intellectual development through encouragement, stimulation and promoting social opportunities.

Family and environmental factors

- **Family history, functioning and well-being:** includes the impact of family situations and experiences.
- **Wider family:** includes the family's relationships with relatives and non-relatives.
- **Housing, employment and financial considerations:** includes living arrangements, amenities, facilities, who is working or not, and the income available over a sustained period of time.

Social and community resources

- **Neighbourhood:** includes the wider context of the neighbourhood and its impact on the baby, child or young person, availability of facilities and services.
- **Accessibility:** includes schools, day-care, primary health care, places of worship, transport, shops, leisure activities and family support services.
- **Characteristics:** includes levels of crime, disadvantage, employment, levels of substance misuse and trading.
- **Social integration:** includes the degree of the young person's social integration or isolation, peer influences, friendships and social networks.

> ### Activity 5.1
>
> ...ove material and make a note of those elements that are less familiar to you. Make sure ...ake time soon to discuss these in supervision or with your manager to help you understand them and integrate them into your practice.

Developmental theories and resources

The importance of reflective practice whilst undertaking work with children and young people cannot be emphasised enough. In the process of using measures of human growth and development it is crucial. This is because children and young people are constantly changing as are their circumstances. This requires a high level of concentration and alertness to changes that will be unique and unpredictable, as well as changes that appear to conform to a predictable developmental transition. Such changes may have nothing to do with your preventive or supportive intervention and some may have everything to do with it. The key is in appreciating that developmental issues are significant and require workers to have a good grasp of them (Thompson, 2002).

The following aims to help the harnessing of these intellectual resources in deciding what to do in working with troubled children and young people. Summaries of the key elements of human growth and development theoretical resources relevant to your assessment task are assembled below. They have been simplified to aid clarity and comparison and should be seen as part of a wide spectrum of potential, rather than deterministic, interactive causative factors in the genesis of problems. Some social psychologists criticise the emphasis in child development theories on normative concepts and suggest enhancing the judging, measuring approach towards one that embodies context, culture, and competencies (Woodhead, 1998). The following summaries should be adapted to every individual situation encountered and always considered against the white, Eurocentric perceptions they embodied when first constructed (Walker, 2003).

Eriksen's psycho-social stages of development

Five of Eriksen's eight stages of development will be considered:

Year 1: The infant requires consistent and stable care in order to develop feelings of security. Begins to trust the environment but can also develop suspicion and insecurity. Deprivation at this stage can lead to emotional detachment throughout life and difficulties forming relationships.

Years 2–3: The child begins to explore and seeks some independence from parents/carers. A sense of autonomy develops but improved self-esteem can combine with feelings of shame and self-doubt. Failure to integrate this stage may lead to difficulties in social integration.

Years 4–5: The child needs to explore the wider environment and plan new activities. Begins to initiate activities but fears punishment and guilt as a consequence. Successful integration results in a confident person, but problems can produce deep insecurities.

Years 6–11: The older child begins to acquire knowledge and skills to adapt to surroundings. Develops sense of achievement but marred by possible feelings of inferiority and failure if efforts are denigrated.

Years12–18: The individual enters stage of personal and vocational identity formation. Self perception heightened, but potential for conflict, confusion, and strong emotions.

Freud's psychosexual stages of development

Year 1: The oral stage during which the infant obtains its' principle source of comfort from sucking the breast milk of the mother, and the gratification from the nutrition.

Years 2–3: The anal stage when the anus and defecation are the major sources of sensual pleasure. The child is preoccupied with body control with parental/carer encouragement. Obsessional behaviour and over-control later in childhood could indicate a problematic stage development.

Years 4–5: The phallic stage, with the penis the focus of attention is the characteristic of this psychosexual stage. In boys the oedipus complex and in girls the electra complex are generated in desires to have a sexual relationship with the opposite sex parent. The root of anxieties and neuroses can be found here if transition to the next stage is impeded.

Years 6–11: The latency stage, which is characterised by calm after the storm of the powerful emotions preceding it.

Years 12–18: The genital stage whereby the individual becomes interested in opposite-sex partners as a substitute for the opposite-sex parent, and as a way of resolving the tensions inherent in oedipul and electra complexes.

Bowlby's attachment theory

The following scheme represents the process of healthy attachment formation. Mental health problems may develop if an interruption occurs in this process, if care is inconsistent, or if there is prolonged separation from main carer.

Months 0–2: This stage is characterised by pre-attachment undiscriminating social responsiveness. The baby is interested in voices and faces and enjoys social interaction.

Months: 3–6: The infant begins to develop discriminating social responses and experiments with attachments to different people. Familiar people elicit more response than strangers.

Months 7–36: Attachment to main carer is prominent with the child showing separation anxiety when carer is absent. The child actively initiates responses from the carer.

Years 3–18: The main carers absences become longer, but the child develops a reciprocal attachment relationship. The child and developing young person begins to understand the carers needs from a secure emotional base.

Piaget's stages of cognitive development

Years 0–1^{1}/$_{2}$: The sensory-motor stage characterised by infants exploring their physicality and modifying reflexes until they can experiment with objects and build a mental picture of things around them.

Years 1^{1}/$_{2}$–7: The pre-operational stage when the child acquires language, make pictures, and participates in imaginative play. The child tends to be self-centred and fixed in their thinking believing they are responsible for external events.

Years 7–12: The concrete operations stage when a child can understand and apply more abstract tasks such as sorting or measuring. This stage is characterised by less egocentric thinking and more relational thinking-differentiation between things. The complexity of the external world is beginning to be appreciated.

Years 12–18: The stage of formal operations characterised by the use of rules and problem-solving skills. The child moves into adolescence with increasing capacity to think abstractly and reflect on tasks in a deductive, logical way.

A more recent view of personality development lists five factors that combine elements of the older more classic ways of understanding a child or adolescent together with notions of peer acceptability and adult perceptions (Hampson, 1995; Jones and Jones, 1999):

- **Extroversion** includes traits such as extroverted/introverted, talkative/quiet, bold/timid.
- **Agreeableness** based on characteristics such as agreeable/disagreeable, kind/unkind, selfish/unselfish.
- **Conscientiousness** reflects traits such as organised/disorganised, hardworking/lazy, reliable/unreliable, thorough/careless, practical/impractical.
- **Neuroticism** based on traits such as stable/unstable, calm/angry, relaxed/tense, unemotional/emotional.
- **Openness to experience** includes the concept of intelligence, together with level of sophistication, creativity, curiosity and cognitive style in problem-solving situations.

Attachment behaviours and patterns in children and adolescents

Secure and autonomous patterns

Infant

Parents and carers of secure infants tend to be good at reading their children's signals. There is synchrony between them involving mutual reciprocal interactions. Clear patterns begin to be perceived by infants that help them to make sense of their own and their parent or carer's behaviour. A parent or carer who is available emotionally, responsive and comforting can generate a soothing, comfortable environment which:

- Helps infants locate and support their own understanding of their own and others' emotions and behaviour.
- Enables the child to access, acknowledge and integrate their thoughts and the full range of their feelings.
- Allows the child to acknowledge the power of feelings to affect behaviour.

Child

Instead of using crying, following and protesting to signify emotional arousal and distress, the young child begins to learn to deal with their feelings cognitively using language and mental processes. Emotional competence develops so that secure children show good affect recognition. The child has increasing confidence in acknowledging and managing difficult and anxiety-provoking emotions.

Secure children function well in family life, classroom behaviour and in peer relationships as they are:

- Reasonably co-operative, and able to draw upon a range of strategies to cope with the demands of social relationships.
- Able to show less emotional dependence on teachers and are more likely to approach teachers in a positive manner.
- Generally popular with their friends. They show good empathy, tend to be included in group activities and show low levels of conflict in their play.
- Less likely to be victimisers or victims, have higher self-esteem and skilled at conflict resolution.

Adolescent

Secure autonomous adolescents acknowledge the value and impact of attachment relationships. The influence of such relationships on personality development is recognised as:

- They can tolerate imperfection in themselves, their parents and those with whom they are currently in close relationship.
- They are able to provide specific, concrete examples that are coherent and reflective when describing attachment experiences.
- They remain constructively engaged with a problem rather than attempting to avoid it or becoming angry at its apparent intractability. And they feel comfortable with closeness, enjoy good self-esteem.

Avoidant-dismissing patterns

Infant

Carers who feel agitated, distressed or hostile towards their infants are less likely to respond to the infants' own distress. They may try to control the situation by ignoring the baby or try to convince the infant they are not 'really' upset. This undermines the child's confidence in their own perceptions. The pattern that develops is that the parent/carer becomes emotionally less available and psychologically distant. They withdraw when the child shows distress and indeed are more available the quieter the infant. In turn the infant learns to become subdued and downplay feelings of upset, need or arousal in order to remain in emotional proximity to the carer.

Child

Avoidant children are less likely to seek support from their carers or teachers. Their attachment style becomes more detached, cool – even socially acceptable. They have learned that their carers feel more comfortable with behaviour that is low in emotional content. Achievements are valued more highly than emotional closeness. Avoidant personalities tend to:

- Modify their own behaviour as a way of defending against social rejection.
- Become compulsively compliant with high anxiety levels in getting tasks 'right'.
- Feel responsible, unsettled, ashamed or guilty if parents or teachers display unhappiness or disapproval.

Adolescent

Avoidant dismissing patterns can be demonstrated ranging from being socially reserved to being compulsively self-reliant. They tend to minimise the emotional effects that relationships have on them. There is if anything a systematic avoidance of negative experiences and memories. The adolescent has a strong need to keep focused on practical tasks. Anything or anybody who distracts them will make this adolescent feel agitated, anxious or angry. Aggressive behaviour is likely to erupt at these moments. Equally this adolescent is keen to keep to the rules and seems over-vigilant when other people appear to break rules. Thus a heightened sense of justice, right and wrong can be observed.

Ambivalent-preoccupied-entangled

Infant

Carers who are inconsistent with their babies needs are experienced as unpredictably unresponsive. Infants feel emotionally neglected and when they begin to explore and seek independence their parents or carers feel uncomfortable. These infants have to increase attachment behaviours in order to break through the lack of carer responsiveness. The infants' behaviour is characterised by crying, clinging, making constant demands and shouting or tugging. Separation anxiety may be pronounced. The parent is in behavioural terms 'non-contingently responsive' – i.e. their responses bear no relation to the behaviour of the child.

Thus the clinging, demanding behaviour increases as the infant learns that persistence will gain a reaction. However, this might be a biscuit or a physical assault. So the infant compensates by becoming hyperactive, maximising the opportunities to gain comfort and attention whenever the carer feels able to provide it. The infant begins to construct a self image with feelings of worthlessness, not being liked or valued. This leads to feelings of doubt, despair and inadequacy.

Child

As the child increases in age it can raise the level of demands and persistence. A parent may threaten to leave the home or request the child to be looked after by the local authority. This only further increases the child's levels of distress, anger and despair. Alternatively where severe physical neglect occurs a child may lapse into passivity, helplessness and depression.

Family relationships can be characterised by high levels of active, demanding behaviour by parents and children. Threats and counter-threats are traded about who cares and who loves who in an impulsive, disorganised atmosphere. Relationships feel emotionally entangled and enmeshed with parents and children learning to lie, deceive and coerce to survive.

Ambivalent children show poor levels of concentration. They might suggest they are feeling unwell in an unspecified way in order to secure a socially acceptable attachment. They are characteristically lacking in self-reliance, failures are always the fault of others, and they see themselves as perpetual victims. These children quickly become known to teachers.

Adolescent

In adolescence the more extreme coercive behavioural strategies become increasingly disruptive, attention-seeking and difficult to control. Life is lived at a heightened pitch of dissatisfaction and anger. Antisocial behaviour, conflict, control problems and poor concentration are observed. Feelings of guilt and personal responsibility are largely absent.

Parents and peers can be subjected to threats and intimidation to make them respond and provide. There is a struggle taking place between anger with, and seeking approval from, parents. These adolescents exhibit a need to be close but to be dependent on someone who may abandon them, arouses strong feelings of anxiety. They feel a strong sense of powerlessness and describe parents, carers and practitioners as either wonderful and loving or hateful and cruel – no shades of grey. However:

- Within these generalised characteristics there is a range.
- Some children are reserved and show mildly avoidant-dismissing patterns.
- Some children are prone to reactive characteristics with mildly ambivalent-preoccupied patterns.
- Don't be fooled by first impressions.
- These classifications are based on white ethno-centric assumptions.
- The original research omitted to distinguish between girls and boys differentiated socialisation.
- Poverty, unemployment, homelessness are important mitigating factors.
- The effects of sexual, physical or emotional abuse can be mistaken for attachment problems.

The Framework for the Assessment of Children in Need 2000

The Framework for the Assessment of Children in Need (DoH, 2000) is the most comprehensive guidance to emerge following implementation of the Children Act 1989. Since 2001 all referrals to social service departments concerning children in need have been assessed under these guidelines in two ways. An initial assessment where the needs are considered to be relatively straightforward, such as a request for family support, a comprehensive assessment and a core assessment:

- **Initial assessment:** this provides a good basis for short term planning and can be used as part of eligibility criteria to determine the level of need and priority. In child care situations it is used to effect immediate child protection with a general requirement of a two week time limit.

- **Comprehensive assessment:** this takes over from where an initial assessment finishes and where more complex needs have been identified. Or it has been initiated following changes in a service user's situation where basic, but limited information already exists.

- **Core assessment:** this is used in child care cases and is a specific requirement under the Children Act 1989 guidance for a time-limited assessment in order to help inform the decision-making process in legal proceedings where the needs are perceived to be more complex, involving a number of concerns about emotional development or child abuse. The key aim is to enable all stakeholders to contribute as much information consistent with effective outcomes.

Activity 5.2

Together with a colleague discuss your experiences of the framework for assessment for 20 minutes. Come up with three improvements you would like to make and present them to your next team meeting.

A recent research project found evidence that workers find the assessment framework cumbersome, over-reliant on prescribed formats, and expected to be undertaken in unrealistic timescales (Corby, Millar and Pope, 2002). The researchers found evidence that parents involved in these assessments felt their views were not being taken sufficiently into account. Key to parental satisfaction with the process was:

- Feeling that their perceptions about their children were taken into account.
- Reaching agreement about the nature of the problem.
- Maintaining optimism and a degree of sensitivity.
- Using the framework flexibly and creatively to maximise parental empowerment.

The principle underlying the assessment framework is that staff need a framework for understanding and helping children and families which takes into account *the inner world of the self and the outer world of the environment*, both in terms of relationships and in terms of practicalities such as housing. This can be called an ecological, holistic, or psycho-social approach. The framework uses a triangular model to distinguish the elements of the assessment framework: the child's developmental needs, parenting capacity, and family and environmental factors. Within each of these elements described more fully in Chapter 3, practitioners are expected to gather specific information for analysis.

Successful implementation of the framework requires you to have a good grasp of the principles underpinning the framework and an ability to translate these principles into practice (Horwath, 2002):

- Assessments should be child-centred and rooted in child development.
- Professionals should recognise and work with diversity.
- Assessment practice means working whenever possible, with children and families and building on the family strengths as well as identifying difficulties.
- The quality of the human environment is linked to the development of the child.
- A range of professionals are the assessors and providers of services to children in need, therefore assessments should be multidisciplinary.
- Assessment is a continuing process meaning interventions and services should be provided alongside the assessment.
- Effective assessment practice is dependent on the combination of evidence based practice grounded in knowledge with finely balanced professional judgement.

Recent research demonstrates that child protection assessments can become dominated by the agenda of social services departments thereby undermining the concept of inter-agency co-operation (Howarth, 2002). Also in the drive to complete recording forms within specified timescales anti-oppressive practice lacks attention, while the pace of the assessment is inconsistent with the capacity of the family to cope. This means already stressful situations can become unbearable.

Activity 5.3

Write down the ways in which you think the guidance will help in your assessment of a child and family you might be working with, and the ways in which this guidance will hinder the assessment.

Commentary

Such a comprehensive guidance framework can seem daunting to staff working under pressure on their available resources. Time is crucial in many situations and it is often difficult to obtain full information in risky circumstances. Interventions undertaken in one set of circumstances can impact on the quality of subsequent assessment – and vice versa. It is important to consider the purpose of assessment and the relationship between assessment and intervention, which can make it hard to separate their functions. The danger is that you might well feel impelled to conduct lengthy detailed assessments following the framework rigidly rather than using it as a guide to practice across a multitude of different circumstances. The skill will be in focusing on the most important aspects of the framework relevant to particular situations.

The social construction of risk

Risk is an inherent part of safeguarding children and young people. Definitions of concepts such as risk, dangerous and significant harm are ambiguous and widely agreed to be determined by social, cultural and historical factors. There is no absolute definition of dangerousness that is independent of any social and cultural context. Similarly, the definition of significant harm is relative. The legal debates about the acceptability of physical chastisement (smacking) of children, is an example of this. In some European states this is illegal it is currently not in England and Wales although there is an ongoing debate about whether it should be so. Many consider such parental behaviour to be physical abuse with the potential for significant harm to the developing child, others believe that sparing the rod spoils the child. This lack of absolutes and the ambiguity it brings has profound implications for safeguarding practice in relation to risk. This is epitomised in the tension between care and control.

Activity 5.4

Make some brief notes describing several disadvantages of viewing risk solely as danger and intervention as about risk control.

Commentary

Ironically the danger of such practice is that in pursuing the ultimately unattainable goal of entirely risk free practice workers may:

- **Overlook the risks attached to intervention:** removing a child allegedly in danger from its family opens the child up to other dangers which can be equally damaging such as developmental or emotional trauma, or scapegoating in foster homes.

- **Lose sight of the individual-in-context, their strengths and the creative potential for development and growth this brings:** focusing too narrowly on one aspect of the individual (e.g. dangerousness) may limit opportunities for interventions that can enable clients to build on their strengths to become less dangerous.

- **Overlook the risk to the worker:** over-eagerness to control risks posed to others can expose workers to unacceptable levels of risk to themselves. This can result not only in serious harm to the worker, but add to the guilt and other problems experienced by the client involved in violence against the worker.

The benefits of the risk management perspective are that they are in keeping with the values of modern practice emphasising the process of *maximising benefits as well as minimising risks* rather than a procedural approach to identifying and eliminating risk. The advantage is that this builds on strengths, the drawbacks are that it relies heavily on highly developed professional competence and judgement and requires the commitment of the client to partnership. It also requires intellectual or cognitive competence of the client. It involves ambiguity and uncertainty, is poorly understood by the public and requires supportive management practice and organisational policy. Risks to workers are virtually ignored. As understanding and practice in relation to risk develops it becomes clear that there needs to be an integration of the best of both approaches. Eliminating or totally controlling risk in child protection work is impossible. It is undesirable to think of risk and the task of safeguarding children in relation to it in this way because:

- Evidence and intuition suggests it is impossible and thus resources are wasted.
- Risk is part of social life.
- Practice which is effective in terms of promoting individual responsibility and social competence can not be reductionist – it must recognise the person in context and build on strengths.
- All agencies have responsibilities in law in relation to certain client groups, Individual workers must neither neglect these responsibilities nor accept unlimited liability – whether or not there are legal requirements.
- The social and individual costs of control can outweigh the social and individual benefits.
- Safeguarding children routinely brings its practitioners into contact with dangerous people and entails professional judgements which are potentially castigated by management, organisations and the media.

It is possible to minimise risk. For example by appropriately employing well validated risk assessment scales where they are available. Other ways of minimising risk would include being aware of the meaning of risk and its role in the personal development and social life of service users. Ensuring practice is evidence based and in accordance with statute, government guidance and agency policy. Managing decision calls – don't be rushed, ensure immediate safety of all parties involved, be appropriately assertive, and be sure a decision has to be made and by whom. The capacity to share responsibility, involve where possible and support the subject of the decision, report back to referring agency, ensure continuity, and debrief as soon as possible with your manager or supervisor is important.

Clearly identifying specific risks and the contexts in which they might occur is a helpful skill to develop. Fully engaging clients and significant others in risk assessment, management and recording accurately is crucial. Multidisciplinary sharing of risk management with other involved professionals while clearly recording risk assessment and management plans, relating them to specific legal requirements as appropriate is necessary. You should always ensure the availability of supervision and recording key decisions from it. Finally never forget that managing risk to self is a priority of professional practice.

Assessment – stage or process?

Whether assessment should be regarded as a stage or part of the ongoing process of intervention is clarified in a recent DoH publication on the working of the Children Act. It asserted that the provision of appropriate services should not await the end of the assessment but be offered when they are required by the child and family. 'The process of engaging in an assessment should be therapeutic and conceived of as part of the range of services offered' (DoH, 2000). Other findings from SSI inspections on assessment and decision making in child care which reflect the generic issues discussed before.

For example, staff did a great deal of fact gathering, but were less good at structuring facts and drawing conclusions from them. It was difficult to discern how decisions were reached on the basis of the information recorded. Decision making needed to be more explicit with plans flowing logically from the assessment. In responding to referrals, social workers followed local custom and practice rather than agency procedures. It was found that the child protection register is not consulted for 60 per cent of children for whom there is some child protection concern. Referrers were not notified of the outcome of their request for services causing confusion and anxiety. Decisions affecting families' welfare were not formally conveyed to them and managers did not sign the case record to indicate their endorsement of the worker's action.

The implications of these shortcomings for the effective management of risk in your agency context are important. Decision making needs to be more explicit. Plans should flow logically from the assessment. There is a need for a guiding agency framework. If decisions are not clearly linked to the findings of assessment, accountability for actions is difficult to support. In the event of unsuccessful outcomes there is no way of analysing which aspect of the situation could account for this and how future interventions could be amended in the light of it. Following local custom and practice rather than agency procedures leads to inconsistency in practice, and is therefore open to complaint from service users on the grounds of inequity of treatment, and is in any case insupportable in terms of professional accountability.

Competent practice in risk work should:

- Adopt a systemic, holistic perspective on need as well as identifying risk.
- Appropriately employ well validated criteria of risk within a coherent framework of assessment and consequent, clearly related intervention.
- Explicitly involve parents and children, recording their perceptions and opinions.
- Avoid gender bias in assessment, recommendation and intervention.
- Utilise multi-disciplinary processes of assessment and decision-making.
- Be explicitly shared in supervision, recorded and endorsed at every stage by managers.

Key Chapter Points

- The *Common Core of Skills and Knowledge for the Children's Workforce* is an attempt to enhance integrated practice in safeguarding children. The main elements of the common core in which people who work with children and young people need to know about and become proficient in are: communication, child development, collaborative practice, supporting transitions, safeguarding and information sharing.

- Government guidance indicates that the Common Assessment Framework (CAF) should be the main and sometimes only assessment instrument to be used at the first sign of emerging vulnerability, and to act as a marker for referral to another agency or specialist service.

- The concept of the *Common Assessment Framework* is that this should lead to a common approach to needs assessment, as an initial assessment for use by statutory or voluntary sector staff in education, early years, health, police, youth justice or social work.

- The importance of reflective practice whilst undertaking work with children and young people cannot be emphasised enough. In the process of using measures of human growth and development in assessment work it is crucial. Thus good practice requires flexible use of these universal measures adapted to the ethnic and cultural context where they are applied.

- Attachment behaviours and patterns in children and adolescents are an important indicator of their emotional and psychological welfare. They should be used as part of a multi-factorial assessment and provide indicators where family or parental support can be targeted.

- The benefits of the risk management perspective are that they are in keeping with the values of modern practice emphasising the process of *maximising benefits as well as minimising risks* rather than a procedural approach to identifying and eliminating risk.

Chapter 6

The Process of Protection

Learning Objectives

- Understand the importance of clear planning and co-ordination for safeguarding children and young people.
- Be clear about the stages of the child protection process and the legal framework supporting it.
- Develop competence in using the provisions of the Children Act 1989 to safeguard children and young people.
- Understand the ways in which the Human Rights Act 1998 can be used to support the welfare of children and young people.

Planning is one of the areas identified in a number of child protection inquiries as a weakness in current practice. The ability to contribute towards and construct an effective child protection plan is a critical part of the process of intervention. In order to be effective planning and intervention needs to be supported by appropriate resources, agreed with parents and carers, realistic and regularly reviewed. At each stage of the process of intervention specific targets and changes need to be established to provide families with clear aims and professionals with clear measures of progress. The process of protection should begin with effective prevention.

A recent research report (DfES, 2004) highlighted specific means for improving effective prevention strategies in safeguarding children and young people. Benefits envisaged include:

- Integrated working with optimal balance between statutory and voluntary provision.
- Greater efficiency to avoid resources being depleted trying to manage entrenched problems.
- Improving user involvement so that children's services augment families own natural coping mechanisms.
- Clarity about which services best meet the needs of different groups of children.

The importance of building a reliable evidence base is crucial to implementing an effective preventive strategy for safeguarding children and young people. Local authorities have to be clear about what it is they are trying to prevent before they can undertake the work. New services need to be designed, implemented and evaluated to meet the specific challenges identified. This might mean the de-commissioning of ineffective prevention services. Ensuring a needs-led strategy and provision is achieved will mean shifting the direction of budgets.

There is some definitional ambiguity surrounding the terms co-ordination, collaboration and co-operation which are found in the child protection literature and often used synonymously. Different authors use these terms to distinguish between the level at which certain activity takes place – such as front line work or managerial level; others relate to the degree of formalisation involved.

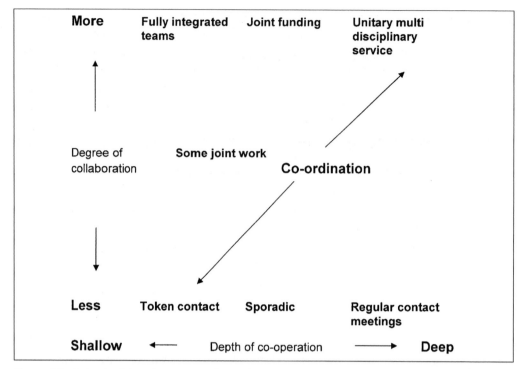

Figure 6.1   Scale of collaboration, co-operation and co-ordination

Some reserve the term co-ordination for the more administrative activities of senior managers while others differentiate along a continuum from minimal collaboration through to full integrated teamwork (Hallett and Birchall, 1992). We discuss these in more detail in Chapter 4. Figure 6.1 illustrates how you might place yourself along such a continuum to measure the degree of working together to safeguard children and young people.

The specific objectives of overall co-ordination are often not specified nor available to empirical testing. The five children's outcomes are sufficiently general and vague to enable government to claim to be tackling child welfare and for service providers to offer examples of success. But will they result in less child deaths or lower prevalence of abuse? And if so can such changes be fully attributable to the new policy environment or other variables unrelated to improvement efforts? Anyway how do you measure improvements in collaboration or co-operation – count up the number of extra meetings or joint visits? The danger is that co-ordination becomes an end in itself, rather than a means to an end. Some attempt has been made to make explicit objectives of co-ordination which resonate with current policy rationales (Challis et al., 1988):

- The achievement of greater efficiency in the use of resources and improved standards of service delivery through the avoidance of duplication and overlap of service provision.
- The reduction of gaps or discontinuities in services.
- The clarification of roles and responsibilities arising in frontier problems and demarcation disputes between professions and services.
- The delivery of comprehensive, holistic services.

The following elements of professional practice will be helpful in sustaining you in difficult circumstances created by risky situations and problems in achieving collaborative care:

- **Good supervision:** this is the foundation of professional practice although practitioners often feel they receive too little. On the other hand you might feel that the kind of supervision being offered is really a management or administrative supervision that is experienced as oppressive. Good supervision attends to the issues related to management of your caseload but equally attends to the emotional and relationship issues that invariably affect your practice. It goes without saying that a profession based on the primary helping relationship requires a model of supervision attuned to the discrete psychological processes at work within you as you experience stressful and distressing assessment situations.

- **Reflective practice:** at its basic this is about learning from our mistakes. But it can be more useful to extend this concept and use it more actively during the process of your assessment work with service users. In other words reflecting about what you are doing as you are doing it. It also involves reflecting back on a piece of work ideally with a colleague or supervisor and evaluating what happened and what you might have done differently. We shall return to this subject throughout this book.

- **Stress management:** contemporary child protection practice is typified by staff working to high levels of stress on a regular basis. Sometimes this is mitigated by supportive colleagues and a thoughtful supervisor, however it is worth considering adopting some self preservation strategies as you begin to experience the demands and pressures of the job. An important factor is stress management. There are whole texts on this subject but for now it is important to recognise this need particularly in the context of your assessment work because so much else hinges on the quality of this work and the consequences that flow from it. There is considerable pressure to get it right, yet we can acknowledge how this is almost an impossible aim. Managing your stress will be as individual as what stresses you, but learning to say no; taking time out; time management; planning your work; seeking supportive supervision; personal insight and relaxation techniques can all help.

The stages of the safeguarding process

Murphy (2004) has identified the stages through which a child protection case may pass. Many cases do not pass beyond the investigation and initial assessment stage. Very few will reach the stage of legal proceedings. The British child protection system has been severely criticised (DoH, 1995) for adopting an approach where many families were included in the system and ejected without a service at an early stage. This drop-out rate can best be explained in terms of the significant harm criteria in the Children Act 1989.

At each stage the system asks whether the child has suffered, or is likely to suffer, significant harm. If the answer is yes, the child proceeds to the next stage. If no, the child drops out of the system. At the same time, if the child is considered to be in extreme danger, at any stage of the process, an Emergency Protection Order may be requested (usually by social services from a magistrate's court) that can remove the child for a short period of time to a safer environment. The series of stages within the child protection system is as follows:

- Observation and recognition
- Referral

- Investigation and initial assessment
- Conference
- Core group, core assessment and review conference

Observation and recognition

The Laming inquiry (2003) discovered several occasions when Victoria Climbié should have been included in the protection system but was effectively excluded by the practitioners who dealt with her. Dingwall et al. (1995) argue that there are certain belief systems that prevent practitioners from recognising the signs of abuse. The most influential of these is *the rule of optimism* which leads to a belief on the part of an individual practitioner that child abuse would not happen in their class, patient list or caseload. A second factor that might hold a practitioner back from acting on a suspicion of significant harm is called *cultural relativism*. This is where the practitioner suspects that something is wrong, but this is excused as normal in that culture, family or community.

In Victoria Climbié's case, the poor relationship between Victoria and her great aunt was reframed as normal in West African families. At some time a threshold will be crossed when the practitioner will begin to suspect abuse and further evidence may then lead to subsequent referral. Often it is difficult for the practitioner to judge if that threshold has actually been passed, in which case it is advisable for the staff member to get help both from within their own agency and from the outside system. Paradoxically, practitioners who have had their awareness of child abuse increased by reading or by training, can express fears that they will employ a *rule of pessimism* and see abuse in every child that they work with (Murphy, 2004).

Referral

The referral stage is often the first stage of inter-agency cooperation and communication, and can set the scene for the interactions that subsequently occur. Referrals can be made to social services, the NSPCC or to the police.

When the referral is made a conflict of expectations sometimes arises. The referrer often comes from a non-social work agency, or is sometimes a member of the family or the public. Making such a referral is an unusual, often stressful event, during which they require reassurance and time to discuss their concerns. But the duty social worker needs to elicit the maximum amount of hard information about the case in order to judge whether it is an appropriate child protection referral or not. Under the *Assessment Framework* (DoH, 2000) the social work team has 24 hours to make an initial assessment, to decide if they should proceed further.

Investigation and initial assessment

The first task of the investigation is to access as much information about that particular child and family. Social services records will always be checked, access to education, health, probation and police information will also be requested. In Britain, police checks reveal if any member of the household has been convicted of serious crimes against children (Schedule 1 offences). If it becomes known that the family had regular contact with any other agency relevant information from their databases would also be sought.

Most agencies have safeguards against disclosure of confidential information to third parties. However, the needs of the child, via the child protection procedures, supersede these safeguards, and relevant information is usually forthcoming. In practice, the test of relevancy and the breaking of confidentiality for some practitioner groups is still an area of some difficulty (Kearney et al., 2000). The gathering of all this information could take a substantial amount of time. There could be a considerable time delay between referral and actual investigative interview. This delay can increase anxiety in the child and the referrer (Murphy, 2005).

Following the gathering of information the investigating social worker interviews sometimes jointly with the police: the referrer; the child; the child's parents or carers; the alleged abuser; the child's brothers and sisters; any other person with relevant information to disclose. Although the interviews with relevant adults may be quite direct and detailed, the interviewers are conscious of the need to form a close working relationship or partnership with the adults who care for the child concerned. When interviewing children, great emphasis is now placed on not leading, suggesting or influencing the child's story in any way (Home Office DoH, 2001).

In British child protection systems, the medical examination commonly occurs in cases of physical and sexual abuse, and sometimes in the cases of neglect, organised and professional abuse. The child always has the right to refuse to be medically examined, and the parent, in some circumstances, also has the right to refuse on their behalf. In practice this refusal seldom occurs. There are three reasons for the investigative medical examination:

- **To inform the system about the likelihood of abuse having occurred.**
- **To gather forensic evidence for use in legal proceedings.**
- **To assess the immediate medical needs of the child.**

There can be significant differences between the medical examinations involved in physical and in sexual abuse. In physical abuse, the medical will frequently be undertaken by a hospital paediatrician. Signs of physical trauma can last for some considerable time but as far as forensic evidence is concerned, the medical examination needs to occur as soon after the abusive event as possible. In child sexual abuse the examination will usually be done by a police surgeon. Forensic evidence in child sexual abuse needs to be gathered as soon as possible, often within 72 hours of the last occasion of abuse.

These investigative medical examinations have been criticised in the past for having been too intrusive (thereby re-abusing the child), and for being too inconclusive, thereby not giving the system any clear messages on which to work. However experienced practitioners can make the medical examination a non-intrusive, positive experience for the child concerned (Murphy, 2005).

The definition of significant harm is not precise and can be adapted to different circumstances. It is the harm which has to be significant – not the act that caused it. Thus a sustained series of privations, not individually harmful as in the case of neglect over time, could amount to significant harm as far as the child's development was concerned. Not all harm will be significant, nor will significant harm in one context necessarily be significant in another. Ultimately it is a matter for the court to determine whether the harm is significant for the particular child in question (Butler and Roberts, 1997).

The child protection conference

The child protection conference is the forum in which the decision about the registration or de-registration of a child is taken and it is the setting where the direction and emphasis of work on a particular case is discussed and formulated. The first significant child protection plan will be established if necessary within this forum. It is also the place where the development of inter-agency conflict or cooperation is established. According to the Department of Health (DoH, 1999) its purpose is threefold:

- To bring together and analyse in an inter-agency setting the information which has been obtained about the child's health, development and functioning, and the parents' capacity to ensure the child's safety.

- To make judgements about the likelihood of a child suffering significant harm in future.

- To decide what future action is needed to safeguard the child and promote their welfare.

The conference draws together all those practitioners and agencies who have, or might have, dealings with the family, as well as the parents and sometimes the children concerned. The ACPC/SCB is a forum for senior managers of agencies, but the conference is a forum largely for practitioners or their first-line managers. Within that forum, it is probable that the four main ACPC/SCB agencies will be represented – health, education, police and social services. The social services department have the task of convening, chairing and minuting conferences on behalf of the system.

Core group, core assessment and review

Following the conference and if necessary, registration stage the core group of workers are expected to form a partnership with the child and family concerned, and to draw up written plans and agreements for the work that will occur within the next six months: The core group is responsible for developing the child protection plan and implementing it. This work will be highly influenced by the *Assessment Framework* and will involve a detailed core assessment of the child's developmental needs, parenting capacity and family and environmental factors. *It should involve a cooperative assessment effort by all the practitioners involved in the core group.* The period allowed for this core assessment under the framework is 35 working days. This timescale is restrictive and is often exceeded.

This period of assessment is also a means of offering assistance to the family to explore the reasons behind the occurrence of the original abuse and to attempt to change the circumstances that led to that abuse. Essentially, therefore, the period is one not just of assessment, but also of consequent therapeutic input: it is where the protective intervention overlaps with the therapeutic one (Murphy, 2005). This assessment period ends with another opportunity for the whole inter-agency group to assess the progress of the work that is being done with the family. The review case conference takes place three months after the original conference or earlier if it is considered necessary and is considered in detail in Chapter 9.

Activity 6.1

Discuss a recent assessment with a colleague or supervisor and reflect back on how you did it. Identify three areas for improvement and the means for doing so.

The Children Act 1989

The Children Act aimed to consolidate a number of child care reforms and provide a response to the evidence of failure in children's services that had been mounting in the 1980s (DHSS, 1985). The Act provides the legislative foundation on which subsequent policy guidance has been built to inform planning and intervention in safeguarding children and young people. There is a specific legal requirement under the Act that different authorities and agencies work together to provide family support services with better liaison and a corporate approach.

The guidance is a key element of the Department of Health's work to support local authorities in implementing *Quality Protects* – the government's programme for transforming the management and delivery of children's social services. This has been incorporated into other government guidance on protecting children from harm, *Working Together to Safeguard Children* (1999), subsequently augmented with the *Every Child Matters* (2003) programme of reforms aimed at developing more effective child protection work and the new Children Act 2004. The duties under the terms of the Children Act 1989 are straightforward and underpinned by the following principles:

- The welfare of the child is paramount.
- Children should be brought up and cared for within their own families wherever possible.
- Children should be safe and protected by effective interventions if at risk.
- Courts should avoid delay and only make an order if this is better than not making an order.
- Children should be kept informed about what happens to them and involved in decisions made about them.
- Parents continue to have parental responsibility for their children even when their children are no longer living with them.

Section 17 lays a duty on local authorities to safeguard, promote the welfare and provide services for children in need. The definition of 'in need' has three elements:

- **The child is unlikely to achieve or maintain, or to have the opportunity of achieving or maintaining, a reasonable standard of health or development without the provision for the child of services by a local authority.**
- **The child's health or development is likely to be significantly impaired, or further impaired, without provision for the child of such services.**
- **The child is disabled.**

The Act further defines disability to include children suffering from mental disorder of any kind. In relation to the first two parts of the definition, health or development is defined to cover physical, intellectual, emotional, social or behavioural development and physical or mental health. These concepts are open to interpretation of what is meant by a 'reasonable standard of health and development', as well as the predictive implications for children having the 'opportunity' of achieving or maintaining it. However it is reasonable to include the following groups of children within this part of the definition of in need and to argue the case for preventive support where there is a risk of children developing problems (Ryan, 1999):

- children living in poverty
- homeless children
- children suffering the effects of racism

- young carers
- children separated from parent/s
- young offenders
- refugee and asylum seekers

Some children from these groups may be truanting from school, getting involved in criminal activities, or have behaviour problems at school or at home. Agency responses tend to address the presenting problem rather than the underlying causes. Assessment of the needs of individual children and families therefore is often cursory, deficit-oriented, and static. It should be more positive, enabling, build on strengths and be undertaken alongside family support measures.

Care orders can be made in respect of children under section 17. This results in the child being placed in the care of the local authority which then assumes parental responsibility for that child. Parents still retain parental responsibility for the child but this is shared with the local authority. The grounds for a care order are:

- The child concerned is suffering significant harm, or is likely to suffer significant harm.
- The harm or likelihood of harm is attributable to:
  - The care given to the child, or likely to be given if the order were not made, not being what it would be reasonable to expect a parent to give them.
  - The child is beyond parental control.

Section 26 provides for a complaints procedure through which children and young people can appeal against decisions reached by social workers. There are informal and formal stages to the procedure with an expectation that an independent person is included at the formal stages. When these procedures have been exhausted a judicial review can be applied for within three months of the decision being appealed against. The three grounds for succeeding with judicial review are:

- **Ultra vires: the social services department did not have the power to make the decision.**
- **Unfair: the decision was reached in a procedurally unfair manner, or by abuse of power.**
- **Unreasonable: all relevant matters were not considered, the law was not properly applied, or there was insufficient consultation.**

Section 27 requires local education authorities and other organisations to assist in functions derived from Section 17.

Section 31 enables staff to apply for a *care order or supervision order* if the child is suffering, or is likely to suffer, significant harm or the likelihood of harm, is attributable to the care being given the child not being what would be expected from a reasonable parent. The court decision is based on the balance of probabilities which means a parent can lose the care of their child even though in a preceding criminal court they were found not guilty because the standard of proof is beyond reasonable doubt.

Section 43 enables staff to apply for a *child assessment order* from a court following parental lack of co-operation in a child protection assessment. The worker in situations like this, and in full care proceedings, has a crucial role in balancing the need to protect the child with the future consequences on them and their family of oppressive investigations and intervention.

Section 44 enables staff to apply for an *emergency protection order* where they need to investigate suspected child abuse and access to the child is being refused. The order allows immediate removal of the child to a place of safety for eight days.

Section 46 permits the police to ***remove and detain*** a child for 72 hours without reference to a court where they have reasonable cause to believe a child would otherwise be likely to suffer significant harm.

Section 47 gives the local authority a ***duty to investigate*** where they suspect a child is suffering or is likely to suffer significant harm. Guidance suggests the purpose of such an investigation is to establish facts, decide if there are grounds for concern, identify risk, and decide protective action.

There is a very extensive body of government policy and practice guidance in relation to assessment in child protection. Several recent reports on assessment in child and family work affirm that many of the general issues about assessment which we have discussed already apply specifically to child care and child protection. Perhaps the most significant is the effects which have been found of the over-emphasis on risk control which followed the Children Act 1989 and various child protection failures. One report concluded that child protection appeared to have a de-skilling effect on staff who were only expecting to respond to families in crisis, and where children were at risk of significant harm. Workers therefore gained little experience beyond this in developing work with families (SSI, 1998). It described a very worrying picture, with departments continuing to respond to child protection and looked after children cases to the exclusion of support to other families of children in need. Therefore too narrow a focus on danger can lead to neglect of the wider picture whereas, a strategy of risk management which takes the wider context into account is more likely to effectively meet need.

This is part of a growing recognition that since the Children Act 1989 practice has focused too narrowly on assessment of risk rather than need (of which risk is only a part). In 1996 a national commission of inquiry into the prevention of child abuse recognised the need for a more holistic approach. It included in its definition of child abuse not only direct and acute forms (such as violence) but also indirect forms such as poor housing, family health and poverty (HMSO, 1996). Nonetheless the narrow view of abuse has persisted and has led frequently to a failure to provide supportive services to children and families in need such that (Reder and Duncan, 2003):

- **Over half the estimated 160,000 children subject to child protection enquiries each year receive no further services.**

- **Interagency work is often relatively good at the early stages of child protection enquiries, its effectiveness tends to decline once child protection plans have been made.**

- **Discussions at child protection conferences tend to focus too heavily on decisions about registration and removal rather than on focusing on plans to protect the child and support the family.**

Case illustration

The following case study examines the skills that could be used when developing a safeguarding children plan and reviewing its progress. As a practitioner you have inherited the case from a colleague who has moved job leaving a risky situation in which the mother is finding it difficult to trust anyone.

Ms B is a depressed young Albanian Muslim woman with three children under five years of age exhibiting disturbed behaviour and a 10 year old at Primary School with poor attendance. The family are refugees and have experienced severe trauma in recent years. Her partner, who is ten years her senior has been involved with drug and alcohol abuse and is suspected of abusing her. She is terrified her children will be removed because she is unable to care for them properly or protect them from the violence of her partner. Ms B is hostile to social workers, health visitors and teachers who have expressed concerns about the welfare of all four children. She feels persecuted, does not want any involvement and resents any interference in her life. The child protection plan summary could look something like this:

- Younger children to attend nursery daily.
- Ms B to play with the younger children once a day.
- Ms B to attend domestic violence survivors group.
- Ms B to take 10 year old to school.
- Partner to attend anger management course.
- Partner to attend drug counselling.
- Family network to visit Ms B weekly.

Activity 6.2

Together with a colleague consider the case illustration and map out an action plan, including alternatives and the reasons for them.

Commentary

Whilst the main focus of intervention must be on the care and safety of the children, practitioners also need to engage Ms B by addressing her own needs for safety and protection. She is aware that her partner will harm her if she asks him to leave so she is stuck in an impossible dilemma. If he stays the practitioner will allege she is failing to protect the children, if she tries to make her partner leave she will endanger herself as well as the children. If staff acknowledge this dilemma in an uncritical way without blaming Ms B or by pretending that there is a simple solution, then they are more likely to begin the process of gaining her confidence and working collaboratively rather than coercively.

The context of her culture and religion are important factors in seeking to understand the complexities of her situation. The practitioner needs to be open and direct about this without giving the false impression of knowing how she feels or by signalling discomfort or embarrassment at such sensitive matters. Consideration should be given to employing an interpreter or translator even though she may be able to make herself understood, as this will signal a respectful approach and provide a cultural connection that will be emotionally supportive.

Engaging Ms B in a conversation about her experiences as a wife and mother in Albania and comparing her life with how it is now will open up a rich seam of information which simultaneously can serve a therapeutic purpose. Getting Ms B to list her worries and concerns about the children will enable her to demonstrate that she is a capable mother. Attempts to engage her partner need to be made but not at the risk of inflaming the situation or putting her and the children at greater risk.

The practitioner can then help her consider ways of tackling these worries in small, practical ways before addressing the major issue of her complex relationship with her partner. The review needs to examine every element of the plan, check whether it is happening, which agency is responsible for what element, what impact the intervention is having on each child's development and whether additional needs have emerged or alternative interventions need to be considered. The review should check whether the plan is addressing and meeting each individual child's developmental needs as well as their collective needs as a sibling group.

The review also needs to examine the parenting capacity of Ms B on her own and conjointly with her partner. The wider family context should be explored to see what pattern of relationships exist with a view to encouraging increased supportive contact. If no immediate family exist then a wider definition of 'family' could identify religious, spiritual or social support networks. In a safer environment the children's behaviour may regress and deteriorate so it is important to distinguish these temporary healing experiences from sustained developmental problems due to continued abuse.

Ms B may not be able to manage every aspect of the plan because it feels overwhelming. For example the survivors group may be poorly organised by unskilled people who cannot meet her particular needs. She may be the only Muslim and the target of racist abuse within the group. Thought needs to be given to finding the right group for her particular needs rather than just the first available resource. However she may be succeeding in getting the older child to school and she must be genuinely congratulated for this.

By establishing a solid platform for her to feel supported, empowered and capable of defining her children's needs she will be more likely to feel strong enough to deal with her violent partner. If the situation became more risky then the practitioner would need to confront Ms B with the likely consequences of inaction on her part. However this needs to be done alongside offering maximum support by all agencies involved in a co-ordinated package. Effective review and closure will more likely happen if a collaborative relationship with Ms B has developed which will enable her to seek further help in future if required.

Legal proceedings

Much child abuse involves assault or exploitation of children leading to criminal proceedings. The police can interview and charge in just the same way as with any assault. The Crown Prosecution Service (CPS) can process the case and the court can arrange a hearing. A typical progress of a child protection case through criminal proceedings would involve an originating report (or disclosure) that a crime had taken place. This would be followed by the police interviewing the victim and relevant witnesses, questioning the alleged perpetrator and then possibly charging them with the offence. A report would go to the CPS, who would arrange a court hearing where the perpetrator would be tried and found guilty or not guilty in the normal way.

In practice there are considerable blocks to the successful prosecution of child protection cases in the British legal system. The CPS has a poor record in successfully prosecuting child abusers and custodial sentences are rare due to witness credibility and lack of corroborating evidence. As well as the potential involvement of the criminal law, it is possible to invoke civil care proceedings. The police, the NSPCC and social services departments have the power to ask the court to invoke short-term legal proceedings (the NSPCC, in practice, seldom do so). The NSPCC and social services have the power to ask the court to consider longer-term legal action. The Children Act 1989 attempted to bring together several different pieces of legislation to afford legal protection to abused children. The following two orders are immediately available in risky situations:

Emergency Protection Order

Where a child has been or is likely to be abused and cannot be protected from the perpetrator of that abuse, an Emergency Protection Order (EPO) is applied for by the field social worker in the

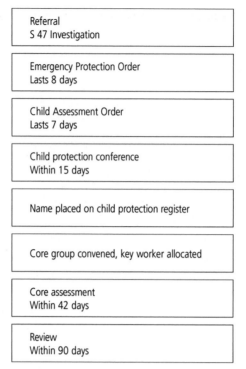

Figure 6.2   Legal process and child protection timescales

Magistrates' court. If granted, the order (which lasts for up to 8 days) enables the social worker to remove the child to any safe, suitable place: this includes the home of a relative, a children's home or a foster family. The order may then be allowed to lapse or may be followed by a series of interim orders until a full care hearing. However under the Family Law Act 1996 new powers were created to permit the exclusion of an alleged abuser from the child's home rather than removing the child.

The EPO may be challenged by parents after 72 hours, and they may choose to challenge all interim orders up to the Care Order. Parents will usually be parties to the proceedings and have the opportunity to be legally represented. The interests of the child will be outlined to the court by a solicitor acting on behalf of an independent worker appointed by the court specifically to discover and then represent the separate interests of the child. The EPO is the route that is used to get immediate protective custody of a child who is seen to be at risk of serious abuse.

Child Assessment Order

However, there is another, less intrusive order that allows the system to assess the condition of a child – a Child Assessment Order (CAO). This order lasts for up to seven days. It is designed to cover those situations where there are concerns about a child, and a lack of co-operation from the child's carers is preventing full assessment. The order is not intended to be used in obviously emergency situations. The effect of the order if granted by a court is to require the child to be produced for assessment under the terms of the order. If the child is of sufficient understanding to make an informed decision, they may refuse a medical or psychiatric examination or other assessment. Use of this order has been minimal since the implementation of the Children Act 1989, demonstrating success in persuading parents to co-operate and reflecting the limited utility of the small seven day timescale.

The Sexual Offences Act 2003

As a result of the Sexual Offences Act (2003) a range of new offences reflecting the modern context of safeguarding children and young people were created:

- New offences designed to tackle all inappropriate sexual activity with children, including causing a child to engage in sexual activity. This is designed to capture behaviour such as persuading children to undress for sexual motives.
- A civil order to apply both to the internet and offline, to enable restrictions to be placed on people displaying inappropriate sexual behaviour towards a child before an offence is committed.
- A new grooming offence with a 10 year maximum custodial sentence.
- A new offence of trafficking young people for sexual exploitation with up to 14 years imprisonment.

Bullying in school

The School Standards and Framework Act 1998 requires that all schools establish an anti-bullying policy, however recent research has confirmed what many parents and welfare agency staff have reported which is that bullying is a major problem and existing strategies within schools are generally inadequate (DfES, 2002). Bullying is a child protection matter as it affects enormous numbers of children and young people making their school experience an unhappy and less effective time for them (NSPCC, 2000):

- 43 per cent of children had been bullied.
- 15 per cent had been physically bullied.
- 10 per cent reported being bullied by an adult.
- 25 per cent of those bullied reported adverse long-term effects.

There is ample evidence of the damage bullying can have on a young person's self-esteem, confidence, ability to learn and sustain relationships. For some the emotional and psychological torment can lead them to commit suicide. Schools are notorious for denying or disguising bullying for fear of attracting a bad reputation, unwelcome inspection and having to admit at failing in their fundamental duty of care to every pupil.

Safeguarding children and young people within school premises means taking bullying seriously, rather than dismissing it as 'part of growing up' or just a variation of horse play and harmless teasing. Teachers and head teachers must take children's complaints about bullying seriously, never dismiss any allegation and recognise the powerful disincentive to report bullying due to the stigma of being regarded as a 'grass' or then further subjected to additional bullying. This emphasises the importance of a pro-active anti-bullying strategy that:

- Understands the secrecy and shame surrounding this issue.
- Being open about acknowledging bullying.

- Having a strong whole-school policy.
- Promoting mediation and conflict resolution.
- Involving pupils in drawing up a school anti-bullying policy.
- Promoting positive relationship skills.

Resources and interventions

We have hitherto mentioned the question of resource allocation (rationing) and its relationship to assessment in safeguarding children and young people. But resource considerations are equally unavoidable when making a care plan and considering what type of intervention to make. In this area too it is impossible to separate out purely practice decisions from resource decisions.

Nevertheless in child protection work you will often encounter those who demand an intervention regardless of whether the resources are available to do it properly. In fact an intervention carried out without ensuring that the necessary resources are available could be considered irresponsible and unethical. All interventions are likely to do some harm so that they are only justified if there are reasonable grounds for believing that the benefits would outweigh the harm. Realistic consideration of the resources available should properly be part of this calculation.

For example placing a 10 year old child with a foster family is a high-risk intervention due to the psychological trauma of removal from the family home and likelihood of placement breakdown. Any decision about whether this is a suitable plan for a child at risk of abuse should take into account not only the child's needs and wishes, but also factors such as:

- Availability of suitable foster families.
- Availability of skilled long-term support available to foster families.
- Availability of skilled intensive input in support of the child.
- Commitment of agency to provide adequate funding to keep this service in place.

If these things are not forthcoming, it might well be the case that this is simply not an appropriate plan for the child and that other arrangements might be preferable. It can be argued that every child has the right to a stable and safe family – and that therefore, regardless of resource considerations, this should be the plan. Our point is that it is not appropriate, or ethical, to lay down fixed rules for practice unless a specific resource context is specified.

For instance, one criticism that can be made of the Laming report into Victoria Climbié's death (Laming, 2003) is that Lord Laming criticises social services departments for not routinely interviewing every child in need referred to them. To interview separately every child in need referred to a social work agency – including those whose need was ostensibly purely a practical need for money or housing – might be desirable. But whether it could or should be made a universal requirement must depend on the amount of social work time that is available and on the competing claims being made on that social work time (Beckett, 2003). Would you want to insist on social workers separately interviewing every child in need referred to their agency if, for instance, this meant taking time away from child protection investigations, or from visiting looked after children?

Activity 6.3

Can you think of instances of interventions which should not be attempted unless adequate resources were secured in advance?

Commentary

You will probably be able to think of other examples, but it seems that some interventions should not be attempted unless the person carrying them out has the necessary skills and training and funding is secured to allow them to bring the process to an appropriate conclusion. What is more they should not be carried out unless adequate support is available to the user of the service, and their carers, during the difficult period while the work is underway.

Time as a resource

While management of financial resources is traditionally the province of managers, day-to-day time management is a task which all practitioners need to take on board. The daily business of juggling competing demands and deciding which to respond to, which to defer and which to decline to meet, may not seem to be the same kind of activity as (say) determining how to spend the financial budget, but it is in essence exactly the same task. Just as managers allocating funds will try to ensure that limited money is used to best possible effect, so the individual worker, deciding how to use their own time, is trying to deployed a limited resource to best effect.

All the same issues that we have been discussing about resource decisions in general occur here, as it were in microcosm. How to respond to crises without squeezing out preventative work? Whether it is right to take a purely utilitarian view or whether there are some calls on staff time that have, on principle, some sort of absolute priority? Indeed, even to describe this sort of decision making as resource management in microcosm is perhaps misleading, as the staff budget is the largest item in any agency's budget, so that effective use of staff time should be the single most important management priority.

However one of the problems that flow from the traditional management-practitioner split is that managers can be surprisingly indifferent to how staff actually spend their time. A worker is given a case but it is not usual for a budget of time to be agreed to deal with the case in the same way that a budget of money would certainly need to be agreed. In fact as has been observed elsewhere, simple arithmetic places very severe restraints on what a worker can do in a given week.

If a worker has 20 cases, they have less than two hours per week to spend on all the visits, telephone calls, recording, travelling, completing forms, going to court and attending meetings that the case requires (Beckett, 2003). That time is just as much a limited resource as money is commonly forgotten. If workers want to spend their agency's money in some new way then it is normal to ask where the money is going to come from and (if the budget is fixed) where savings are going to be made in order to make it available. But this sort of thinking process is often cast aside when it comes to the allocation of time. Additional tasks are given to people who are already fully occupied, the unspoken assumption being that they will fit it in somehow.

This poor practice is the basis of our criticism of the Laming report above. We would suggest that there is no merit in demanding that, for example, social work agencies should routinely interview every child in need referred to them, unless the person making the demand can identify where the time is going to come from. Assuming that additional staff time is not going to be made available, the person making the demand needs to specify what tasks are going to be dropped in order to create time for this new one.

> *Activity 6.4*
>
> Can you think of other examples in your own experience of complex pieces of work which should not be undertaken unless an appropriate amount of time is made available?

Commentary

You may come up with many different examples but generally speaking these will most likely relate to chronic and entrenched difficulties in severely impoverished families. Here the rule of optimism is turned relentlessly into the rule of pessimism – equally as dangerous as it leads often to self-fulfilling predictions from cynical and demoralised staff. Changing the functioning of a family which has, for several generations, been viewed by professional agencies as abusive or neglectful can seem an impossible task with the belief that no amount of resource time will make a difference.

Working to change long-established patterns of behaviour such as drug addiction or sexually abusive behaviour can also seem daunting. Remember however that your feelings of frustration and hopelessness are probably mirrored within the family system and need to be challenged within you as much as within the family. Every family deserves a chance and you may need to re-define what success means into small, realistic, incremental gains rather than unrealistic outcomes. This avoids setting up the parents to fail and may require sustained long term contact with families lacking in many resources.

The Human Rights Act 1998

The Human Rights Act (UN, 1998) came into force in 2000 and incorporates into English law most of the provisions of the European Convention on Human Rights. The Act applies to all authorities undertaking functions of a public nature, including all care providers in the public sector. The Human Rights Act supports the protection and improvement of the health and welfare of children and young people throughout the United Kingdom. *Article 3* concerns freedom from torture and inhuman or degrading treatment. Children and young people who have been subjected to restraint, seclusion, or detention in public care as a result of alarming behaviour could use this part of the Act to raise complaints.

Article 5 concerns the right to liberty, and together with *Article 6* concerning the right to a fair hearing, are important to children and young people detained under a section of the Mental Health Act 1983, the Children Act 1989, or within the youth justice system. Workers involved in such work must ensure that detention is based on sound opinion, in accordance with clearly laid out legal procedure accessible to the individual, and only lasts for as long as the mental health problem persists. In the context of youth justice work, particular attention needs to be paid to the quality and tone of pre-sentence reports which can be stigmatising. The formulaic structure of pre-sentence reports might not enable an assessing social worker working under deadline pressure, to provide an accurate picture of a young person.

Article 8 guarantees the right to privacy and family life. Refugees and asylum seeking families can become entangled in complex legal procedures relating to citizenship and entitlement. This provision can be invoked when UK authorities are considering whether a person should be deported or remain in this country. Compassionate grounds can be used for children affected by the proposed deportation of a parent or in cases where a parent is not admitted. Workers attuned to the attachment relationships of often small children can use this knowledge to support Article 8 proceedings. In such circumstances the maintenance of the family unit is paramount.

Staff involved in care proceedings or adoption work will have to consider very carefully whether such plans are in the best interests of the child but also are consistent with the child's rights under the Convention. For example, the Convention emphasises that care orders should be a temporary measure and that children should be reunited with their family as soon as possible, where appropriate. In the case of a parent with a mental health problem detained in a psychiatric hospital, the Convention could be employed by their children to facilitate regular visits if these have been denied.

Article 10 concerns basic rights to freedom of expression and in the context of children's welfare is a crucial safeguard to ensuring that practitioners work actively to enable children and young people to express their opinions about service provision. Practitioners have an opportunity within this specific provision to articulate and put into practice their value principles of partnership and children's rights.

Article 14 states that all children have an equal claim to the rights set out in the Convention 'irrespective of the child's or his or her parent's or legal guardian's race, colour, sex, language, religion, political or other opinion, national, ethnic or social origin, property, disability, birth or other status.' This provision could be used to argue for equality of service provision and non-prejudicial diagnosis or treatment. Workers need to ensure they are employing anti-racist and non-discriminatory practice as well as facilitating children and young people to:

- **Access information about their rights.**
- **Contact mental health services.**
- **Access advocates and children's rights organisations.**
- **Create children's service user groups.**

However in a damning report by the Children's Rights Alliance for England (2004) it was revealed that the UK government has only made progress in 17 of the 78 recommendations made by the United Nations Committee on the Rights of the Child in 2002, designed to make UK law, policy and practice compatible with the UN Convention on the Rights of the Child.

Key Chapter Points

- The series of stages within the child protection system is as follows: observation and recognition, referral, investigation and initial assessment, case conference, core group, core assessment and review conference.

- The Children Act 1989 attempted to bring together several different pieces of legislation to afford legal protection to abused children. The Act aimed to consolidate a number of child care reforms and provide a response to the evidence of failure in children's services that had been mounting in the 1980s.

- Bullying is a child protection matter and the School Standards and Framework Act 1998 requires that all schools establish an anti-bullying policy.

- While management of financial resources is traditionally the province of managers, day-to-day time management is a task which all child protection practitioners need to take on board.

- The Human Rights Act came into force in 2000 and supports the protection and improvement of the health and welfare of children and young people throughout the United Kingdom.

Chapter 7

Supporting Young People's Transition

Learning Objectives

- Reflect upon the reason for and effects of risk taking behaviour in young people.
- Understand the preparatory work required to support young people through transition from child to adult services.
- Reflect on your changing role with the young person during and after transition.
- Understand the communication issues and opportunities between practitioners and children and young people.

Before the emergence of a youth culture or 'teenagers', boys and girls went directly from childhood to adulthood from school to work at a young age. They were often not able to express their unique identities until they were in a position which enabled free expression, by then most appeared to conform to their role in society and did not appear to openly rebel (Bee, 1992; Bannister and Huntington, 2002). Research has acknowledged the needs of older children and young people which gave rise to studies showing the complexities in the lives of young people and their life style choices (Stokes and Tyler, 2001).

This chapter investigates the ways young people can be seen to be at risk and how they can be supported into adult services, whether leaving care and young offenders units or moving from school to further or higher education, and for some young people moving from child to adult health services. This is relevant for young people in general and in particular for young people at risk. The definition of children is deemed to include all individuals under 18 years of age, young people imprisoned up to their 22nd birthday, young people leaving care either to the age of 21, or until they have completed their full time education, and finally young adults with learning disabilities until 21 years of age, (Children Act 2004) .

The preferred sequence would be for services which would allow all young people to develop their skills of self-management progressively rather than in one large leap. For some young people the process may be about offering them opportunities for greater autonomy and self determination, whether leaving school or local authority care, for others it may be for greater responsibility for managing their long term health condition. Finally for a small minority it may be about finding a suitable place of safety which is able to support a longer transition process, either because the young person is vulnerable or because others may be at risk from the young person.

Challenges for the child and young person

Challenges often commence when the child or young person leaves their home setting and enter school (Taylor and Field, 1997). Once the child adjusts to the school environment the transition from primary to secondary education can highlight further concerns. To begin with, the young person has to go through the changes of adolescence alongside their peers, this can be fraught as young teenagers who are seen as early or late developers can often feel different from their friends and class mates. Taylor and Müller (1995) argue that young adults also have developmental tasks that they are required to achieve as they go through the transition from child to adult. This includes adapting to change in their body and their sexual characteristics, becoming more independent from their family, and developing further adult social skills while working towards expected academic and workforce skills.

Young people at this time in their lives often appear to go through a period of negativity, particularly with parents right at the beginning of puberty; many of these conflicts surround the teenagers need for independence. An enormous amount of evidence from an assortment of tasks shows that adolescents and young adults are capable of feats of reasoning not attained under normal circumstances by younger children, and that these abilities develop fairly rapidly during the age of about 11 to 15 (Neimark, 1982 in Bee, 1992). Finally as part of maturation the young person needs to develop a feeling of self worth as an individual while developing personal beliefs of their own norms and values.

Youth culture is an often spoken word to describe the ways young adults differ from both children and adults in society. The nature of what constitutes culture has been explored and developed over time from a simple sharing of values and beliefs to a complex interaction, which explores the relationship of individuals (Helman, 2001). (This concept is developed in more detail in Chapter 8.) This determines the individual's behaviour, which may vary from society to society. This is dependent on the life and times of the society and may even reflect the status given to children and young adults with regard to their roles and responsibilities in society.

While young people are often seen as a challenge to society's productive and economic outcomes in the short term by not always conforming to the rules, they also hold the hope for the future and are therefore accommodated into the structure of society by being seen as 'going through a phase' usually during their later years in education as they transfer from the world of the child to the world of the adult. Once the young person recovers from this phase it is assumed by society that this will lead the young person on to a productive working life.

This could however lead to potential conflicts for the young person with little or no education or career prospects or the young woman who discovers she is pregnant, or the refugee who is unable to speak English. As society is still often not able to view these individuals as having the ability to pursue productive lives, and while their situation may allow for flexibility in following the rules, it may also restrict the young person's ability to develop their lives further. Stokes and Tyler (2001) in their exploration into the lives of young people go one stage further and argue that young people today live *multi-dimensional lives*. While in the past the outcome following education for most young people would have been similar (job, further education and then for most marriage and family) today the focus is away from education, and is determined by other life concerns which may include family issues, drug related problems, justice and health issues.

Risk taking behaviour

These challenges to develop and adjust to their changing bodies and lives and society's perception of who the young person is, and should be, can be more problematic when other influences are involved in their decision making (Kyngas et al., 1998). Risk taking is seen to carry out behaviour that may end up in disaster, damage or injury. This can be seen as a need by the young person to walk a fine line between fearfulness and exhilaration, even though the young person may only see the thrill and not the risk. Influences that may lead to difficulties include responses by the young person, their family and friends to the developmental responsibilities, and ambiguity in the role of the young person during this time. This is most significant when related to family and how the young person views their place and task within this, and also more broadly the environment the young person lives within including the local community, school and peer groups (Visser and Moleko, 2005). Examples of risk taking behaviour include:

- fighting
- joy riding
- traffic dodging
- drinking alcohol
- taking drugs
- smoking
- vandalism
- hooliganism
- playing truant
- having unprotected sex
- having a baby
- stealing
- burglary
- murder
- prostitution
- becoming homeless
- carrying a gun or knife
- self harm
- attempting suicide
- not complying with treatments for health conditions
- playing extreme sports

The types of risk taking behaviour can be seen to be on a continuum, from staying out late at night, to getting into fights right through to committing murder or trying taking your own life. A degree of risk taking is thought to be a 'normal' transitional behaviour during adolescence, however extreme risk taking can lead to self destructive activities (Visser and Moleko, 2005).

Commentary

Walker (2002) adds to the discussion on risk taking behaviour especially surrounding young people and prostitution whereby young people who lack boundaries set by their parents to supervise and challenge high risk behaviour have more potential to continue the risk taking. She also highlights the positive influences of friends and peers in reducing the involvement in deviant behaviour. Some of the factors cited above such as powerlessness and conflict can be directly linked to previous abuse, however concerns of sexually active young teenagers who are promiscuous is not evidenced in research studies. It is rather the case that few young people have casual sex and multiple partners are rare (Moules and Ramsey, 1998).

Deliberate risk taking behaviours can cause hazardous situations to occur for the young person including physical harm and law breaking which could lead to prosecution and imprisonment. There are also other situations which are not of the young persons choosing, this may be aggression towards the young person in an environment which places them at risk (which can be their local community), and persecution of the young person which may lead on to further abuse. Finally being of a different ethnic group, religion, or sexuality to the majority of individuals around may also place the young person at risk (Garratt et al., 1997).

Belonging to most peer groups involving young people does not encourage rebellious conduct – it often gives the young person a common identity and peer group support. It is society's *perception of young people* that gives the opinion that groups of young people are more likely to cause trouble (Gregg, 1995). Common belief has been that the moral decline of young people who offend was the result of poor parenting, the breaking up of families with the destruction of family values rather than social deprivation and poverty caused by the increase in homes broken by separation or divorce.

Perceptions of young people

Society on the whole does not appear to have a high opinion of teenagers, Garrett et al. (1997) reflect that it is a common view that young people are always involved in crime, violence or drugs (this can be seen in the increased use of ASBOs, Slack, 2005). Young people should however be 'depicted as an oppressed group, openly discriminated against in local and national politics, and who have to struggle, mostly unnoticed, in order to overcome adult prejudice' (Garrett et al., 1997: 1). During adolescence, young people 'will experience change in a number of areas: from child to adult health services, school to higher education or work and childhood dependence to adult autonomy' (SCARE briefing 2004 section 9: 1). This dichotomy on society's negative view of young people and

Mental health issues	Conflict (school, home)
Unhappy home life	Status ambiguity
Physical illness or disability	Powerlessness
Sexual confusion	Peer pressure
Poor role models	Unemployment
Lack of support	Non-conformity
Learning disorders	Lack of information
Living in care	Immaturity
Drug or alcohol abuse	Poverty
Isolation (cultural, geographical)	Social environment
Lack of professional sensitivity	Ill health
Learning disabilities	Stress
Physical abuse	Sexual abuse
Lack of family structure	Permissive parenting
Domestic abuse	Neglect
Inadequate education	Poor fitness

Figure 7.1   Reasons behind risk taking behaviour

the needs they have unfulfilled can also affect the services offered, as individuals may not always be seen as deserving of services which are theirs by right.

The experience of young people acquiring the skills to adapt and survive in adult society is difficult enough as the cultural norms around language, behaviour, and lifestyle seem to shift more quickly than the young person can comprehend or adjust to (Bee, 1994). However when we consider the example of a young person with social issues this becomes more complex. While teenage rebellion around schooling and leisure can be negotiated with family, for a young person in care or young offender unit, this becomes infinitely more difficult. Therefore, the young person is more likely to feel hemmed in by their circumstances which may lead to nonconformity and the potential of increased risk taking behaviour.

Young people who do not conform to society are either challenged in some way or act out their frustrations in a non-socially acceptable fashion. Griffin (1993: 129) argues that 'stories about delinquency juggle the contradictory representations of young people as victims (of other 'delinquent youth', environmental conditions, psychosocial or psychological characteristics), and perpetrators (of delinquent activities)'. Whichever viewpoint becomes the accepted belief young people who offend can be seen as a group of vulnerable individuals who need guidance to develop into mature citizens.

Youths who persistently offend may be problematic but in many ways they often can be seen as a product of society rather than a problem for society to treat. Maybe the observation of every behaviour not seen as normal and therefore delinquent has led these frustrated young people to turn their backs on societal norms because they feel there is no way they can live up to them. Society does not necessarily give these young people many resources to enable them to develop as individuals and they therefore continue to express the views of the whole gang or peer group (Hendrick, 2005).

The fact that some youths persistently offend must mean that even when caught they still receive more benefit by committing the offence than if they were to become law abiding. The seriousness of the offence may reflect their position in their group and indeed may be the only way to stay part of the group. The law abiding youth would have a different method of attaining status, but for these troubled youths it is a way of bonding with their peers. Only by giving positive reinforcements to not commit further offences can it be hoped to break the link in their potential crime career. Community supervision rather than custodial sentencing in youth justice that is well resourced both financially and with experienced professionals has been a positive step forward.

Needs of young people

When exploring the needs and requirements of young people, care has to be taken to acknowledge the variety of situations that may place young people at risk and requiring help from specific services. Some young people are preparing to leave care, others are working with youth offending teams due to criminal behaviour, and some young people are challenged by leaving school and deciding their future, while others are living with abuse or long term health or social needs. Not every young person will be seen to be in need of specific services, however opportunities should be available for all young people to access services which are universal. Issues such as disability, culture and religion also need to be acknowledged.

One of the themes that often appears for children and young people at risk is the difficulties of transition from child and youth services to adult services, or indeed a complete discharge from services when young people leave care. While the individual needs of young people within child and youth services seem to be more in focus, and a clearer picture of the care that needs to be offered compared with the past, this is still not always ideal (Wilson and James, 2002). When preparing young people to transfer to adult services a number of different options may need to be explored related to the specific assessment of the young person's needs.

Support for the young people should change as the transition occurs between child and adult services and once the young adult is receiving services from the adult teams. This includes the success of the communication between services. Child and young people focused services appear on the whole to be able to co-ordinate care between agencies and the specialist services satisfactorily. This seems to be more problematic in the move to adult services. Conway et al. (2000) in their discussion on the Leeds Method of Management for Cystic Fibrosis (known as CF this is a chronic lung condition which is the most commonly inherited condition in the UK) highlighted the reluctance of some adult physicians who deal with chronic lung disease to collaborate in the shared care of individuals. This is often due to the unique needs of young people with CF, which has only within the last 10 years progressed to mainstream adult services due to the increasing life span of adults with CF. Young people may then have to develop strategies to ensure consistent standards of treatment and therefore only communicate with the specialist centres for their treatment rather than use local acute hospital services who are often seen to have gaps in their care management and specialist knowledge. Therefore, as a consequence young people with specific chronic illness have to often fend for themselves with little health professional support when undertaking specific treatment at home especially when an acute episode occurs, (Walters and Warren, 2001).

This is slowly improving and in some geographical locations away from specialist centres nurse specialists are filling in the gaps that occurred on leaving children's services. Other more common long term conditions that young people may live with such as diabetes and asthma, seem to be more successfully handled due to the larger numbers of individuals with the conditions and the larger amount of resources and expertise that is in place both locally and at specialist centres.

Other challenging issues can occur for young people coming of age and leaving care, and also young offenders leaving secure units. The need to support the young adult integrating into their local community, finding appropriate housing and work or education can be hampered by the lack of resources and planning. The principal risk factors associated with teenagers who have been looked after (including young women who become pregnant) and could also relate to young offenders include, 'socio-economic deprivation; limited involvement in education; low educational attainment; limited access to consistent, positive adult support; being . . . a teenage mother; low self esteem; and experience of sexual abuse, which are to be found more often in the looked after population than among children and young people who are not in care' (SCARE Briefing, 2004, 9: 1).

Activity 7.3

What specific assessment issues have to be considered when exploring with the young person in your area of practice their move to adult services?

Would there be further issues for other agencies to explore that you have not included?

Assessment of need

Assessment of the young person's needs is the first step in ensuring that a tailor-made service can be offered. The most straightforward and commonly offered support is exploring options following GCSEs or A Levels, either employment or further education, or considering the availability of programmes to take at university or college. More complicated would be to assess the young person's health needs particularly if they have a long term or chronic illness as this may have a profound effect on their future life style. Young people leaving care will need to have their housing and financial needs assessed to ensure that the young person will not be homeless and living in poverty. Mental health issues also need to be assessed as a number of young people who have depression or stress affecting their mental well being has increased over the last few decades. In terms of anti-discriminatory practice Walker (2003: 17) comments 'it is important that children, families and carers have maximum choice when engaging in services aiming to meet their needs, and as important not to assume that black families only require black staff'.

The way child and youth professionals approach transition for the young person can have long term repercussions, both in the perception the young person has of who they are, but also for the young person's experiences in transferring to adult services. Baker and Coe (1993) in their American discussion on individuals transition to become young adults within health service provision, highlighted the need for professionals to take on board the young person's developmental issues alongside their treatment. This enables the young person to become more independent incrementally, rather than suddenly being expected to undertake all their own care once they reach the age of 16+. This process enables the young person to adapt and readjust with each increasing responsibility offered to them with regard to their care.

The role of the professional when caring for children and young adults therefore varies over time. While supporting, caring and educating the family will be consistent, emotional and psychological support will need to change and adapt to the young adult's needs as they physically and psychologically grow and develop (Casey, 1988; 1993). The guidelines offered (SCARE Briefing, 2004, 9: 1) acknowledge this challenging time for the young person both emotionally and physically. The guidelines urge the professionals caring for the young person to be aware and realistic in the issues that may arise, which may include conflict with parents or professionals working with the young people.

The young person will usually wish to become more independent as they reach their middle to late teenage years, they may also at times have a problem with non-cooperation. These issues may vary from the need to undertake further education and reflect upon career opportunities, to the exploration of adult relationships and the wish to have families. The professional has a requirement to ensure that individual's need for information is also met.

The child or young person will need to make decisions with various degrees of support from their family and professionals depending upon age and level of independence and on-going relationship with family members. Young people leaving care or young offenders units will need further support from professionals as they may lack support from family members to discuss issues. The concerns about inconsistency of support from services may be due to where the young person lives and is also reflected in the support that can be offered by specific youth practitioners whether within youth services, Connexions or youth offending teams.

While some parts of the country have well established teams who offer a service often via specialists who are experts in young people and their needs, there are still a significant number of individuals who have minimal input from specialist youth services unless they are offenders. These young adults who have been involved in the criminal justice system are trying to live as normal a life for themselves as they can, however it is very difficult for them to find and hold down a job or continue in full time education. While this specialised service gives the individual the physical support and an intervention if required, it might not always take into account the uniqueness of the person and their family. In addition, while the opportunity may arise for some individuals the reality is that for many young people the resources are not available in their geographical area. Even when the service is available, the time and financial restraints may make the service difficult to implement. Research with nurse specialists in practice demonstrates this was clearly highlighted (Hernetal, 1998). While nurses and doctor acknowledge the value of progression services for young adults before they reach adult care, practically this is much more difficult to plan.

Garrett et al. (1997: 47) highlight the issues for some young people leaving care 'before I came on the streets I had some support from social services. but once I turned 18 that was it. The care order was off and so far as they were concerned you weren't in their care any more. You were on your own basically. We'll chuck you in a little flat and you survive, goodbye!' It is an essential consideration to assess the needs of all young people regardless of their situation during transition. The Children (Leaving Care) Act 2000 has some specific guidelines which could be generally applied to many situations to improve the transition period into adulthood, taking into consideration the young person's views and concerns.

Pathway plans for the future	A genuine involvement of the young person in developing a plan which considers their hopes and anxieties for the future.
Clear assessment, preparation and planning for transition	Helping the young person to develop relationships and skills which include qualifications in readiness for future career.
Effective personal support following transition	All young people at risk should have their own personal advisers who are the links between the young person and the local agencies.
Accommodation following transition	All young people at risk require a range of tenancies. The agencies should also offer support if the tenancy is unsuccessful.
Inclusive service for young people	Young people with disabilities require personalised service. Individual circumstance will also be acknowledged, including culture, health, ethnicity and religion.
Further education, training and employment	Young people at risk will be encouraged to continue education. Young people at risk will be supported to achieve the level of academic attainment as their peers. Schools should have a designated teacher for young people (especially those in care) and help them to develop a personal education plan (PEP).
Safeguarding young people through advocacy	Practitioners should be offering a listening culture. Support should be available to young people when they make complaints. Young people should be offered specific advocacy services.
Multi agency partnerships	A multi agency approach should be offered focusing on the young person. Offering the young person appropriate services as required.

Adapted from Children (Leaving Care) Act 2000

Figure 7.2 Guidelines for helping young people leaving care

Supporting young people

Guidelines

These guidelines can be used for all young people requiring specific care services whether leaving care, young offenders unit, special education or transferring to adult health services. The notion of having an individual practitioner who will support the young person through the whole process and act as a guide to services and resources available may encourage the young person to feel confident in themselves and their long term future

---

Activity 7.4

Using the guidelines reflect upon how you can utilise them with the young people you work with.
What other elements may need to be added for your service?

Commentary

While the guidelines are a good starting point, there may be specific needs that the young people have relating to their situation. For example the young person may require specific resources or finance organised due to a health condition. They may need specific equipment or modification to their accommodation because of a physical disability. The young person may need continuation of counselling due to abuse or terminal illness. However the work with young people regardless of specific issues has commonalties in respect of the approach taken when offering support. Many ways that young people can be supported during transition are straightforward and discussed below.

Skills for supporting young people's transition

- Active listening.
- Utilising windows of opportunity to discuss issues.
- Offer non judgemental support (including body language).
- Discuss values and beliefs in a safe way.
- Not concentrating on the trivia.
- Focusing on the important issues.
- Offering the young person respect and dignity.
- Ensuring a private place to talk if required.
- Helping young people to reflect on their personal experiences.
- Encouraging the young person to make their own decisions.
- Having a positive attitude.
- Offering a friendly approach.
- Offering opportunities to develop independence especially in relation to health or disability.
- Tailoring resources to meet the needs of young people from different cultures and religions.
- Role modelling working together with other professionals.
- Offering social opportunities as part of the process.
- Having a good sense of humour.

Hollander (2002) comments that the main way that enables young people to feel supported, is honest and open communication which facilitates concerns and issues to be shared in a non-critical, constructive environment. Every young person is unique and therefore transition from specific child services to adult services needs to be tailored to their specific needs. When working in partnership with young people and their families, child and youth practitioners need to ensure openness to their wishes even if it does not reflect the practitioner's own values and beliefs.

To enable young people who are moving to adult services to be as least stressed as possible professionals need to ensure either the full involvement of the family or supportive carers. While some young people may require information and reassurance, others might need longer term support from health professionals, youth offending teams or support groups. Some young people go on to further education, others to work, however some disaffected young people may have issues and concerns which may reduce their success in finding a job, developing adult relationships or even having a roof over their heads. These are the young people who will continue to have input from the caring professions. If during transition, services offered are clear and well resourced and with good networking across agencies, then this may ensure that young people reach the potential they strive to achieve.

Key Chapter Points

- The perception of young people and their needs was explored, focusing on the physical, developmental and personal changes that occur.
- The reason and effects of risk taking behaviour in young people highlighted the environmental, family and emotional issues involved.
- Exploration of the preparatory work uncovered the support young people require financially, physically and emotionally.
- The changing role of the professional requires the facilitation of an incremental progression of the young person to independence.
- Society's view of young people is predicated on the negative perceptions that occur and the issues this causes.
- The needs of young people were investigated showing the gaps in services.
- Guidelines for supporting young people in transition explored how the gaps in service may be filled using youth-friendly services.
- Communication skills and opportunities for discussion between practitioners and young people brought to light the need to be open minded, supportive and non-judgmental.

Chapter 8

Social Inclusion and Cultural Competence

Learning Objectives

- Describe what is meant by social inclusion and cultural competence.
- Illustrate the importance of anti-discriminatory practice for safeguarding children and young people.
- Explain what changes can be made to contemporary practice to meet the needs of a diverse society.
- Describe the elements of socially inclusive safeguarding practice.

Social disadvantage, unemployment, bad housing and impoverished surroundings are among the characteristics of socially excluded families and indicate risk factors for child abuse. However, poverty does not cause child abuse and it is very important not to generalise or stereotype families struggling with multiple challenges. Indeed evidence demonstrates that child abuse occurs in wealthier families where it is easier to conceal and avoid scrutiny. It is important therefore to consider the needs of children and families who are at risk and identify preventive measures to reduce the risk of child abuse happening in the first place. Socially excluded families are under the most stress under circumstances beyond their control therefore it is important to target resources on support and prevention. This in the long term is preferable to reacting to incidents of abuse.

The concept of social exclusion has its origins in France in the 1970s where the idea of citizenship and social cohesion highlighted the plight of *Les exclus* who were relegated to the margins of society (Barry and Hallett, 1998; Pierson, 2002). Social inclusion is the social policy aimed at enabling each individual regardless of class, race, culture, age, religion, disability or gender to surmount the traditional barriers to their advancement so that nobody is excluded from sharing in the wealth and resources of the country.

These political aspirations fit with the value base of safeguarding children and young people which embody anti-discriminatory practice, partnership, and equal opportunities for every citizen. However evidence suggests that such aspirations are difficult to change the structural, entrenched attitudes and beliefs that continue to discriminate against minorities (Leonard, 1997). Staff concerned with safeguarding vulnerable children are among those in the front line faced with the consequences of the failure of social inclusion measures and the raised expectations of families in need.

Evidence suggests that the process of exclusion continued in the 1970s as rising levels of poverty began to be quantified (Walker, 2001a). In the process a new role has evolved for statutory child protection as a front-line service focused on the management of exclusion and rationing of scarce resources (Jones, 1997). This has always been an uncomfortable position for those who subscribe to an empowering model of practice that seeks to challenge social injustice.

The evidence confirms that the gap between rich and poor is widening, there are more children living in poverty, the prison population is at its highest recorded level, and disabled people are more likely to live in poverty or be unemployed than non-disabled people. Children from working class families are less likely to receive a further or higher education and black families are more likely to live in poor housing. Both have disproportionate numbers of children and young people on the child protection register (NCH Fact File, 2000).

Recent budgets planned to focus on creating a 'family friendly' welfare environment with a mixture of income support, access to child care, and parental leave entitlements that are beginning to resemble some of the other progressive European countries. However the UK still sustains shameful levels of child poverty which are a serious impediment to improving the life chances and protection of every child and young person. The national Sure Start programme and subsequent development of Family Centres are part of the mosaic of preventive services being built around the needs of children.

Youth work still languishes at the bottom of social policy priorities with few resources despite growing evidence of the positive impact it can make with disadvantaged, disaffected and troubled young people. The review of youth services and the consultative green paper in 2005 still predominantly reflected government pre-occupation with viewing young people as potential miscreants requiring control and direction, rather than as a heterogeneous, diverse population many of whom have been or are, suffering abuse and neglect. However these new social policy developments seen as a whole are a useful input into the matrix of service changes in the community that have the potential to assist you in your safeguarding practice.

Child protection in the community

The Commission of Inquiry into the Prevention of Child Abuse (1996) identified the promotion of a child-friendly community through community development as one of the overarching means of preventing child abuse. A number of factors were identified as important to the care and welfare of children:

- The degree of social integration and isolation.
- Imbalances of power.
- Social attitudes towards children.
- Levels of awareness of children's needs.

In 2004 the number of children permanently excluded from school increased by six per cent. Research indicates that pupils with special educational needs are four times more likely to be excluded from school, while black pupils are more than twice as likely to be excluded compared with white pupils. There is strong evidence of a link between school exclusion and future criminal activity given the lack of resources outside the formal education system (NCB, 2005). Under the current league table competitive system some head teachers are exporting children with problems and arguing against the policy of inclusive education for children with special needs.

The idea of community development is based on the premise that most people's problems are sorted out within and between their existing local network of friends, relatives and neighbours. You have a role in seeking to reinforce and support those networks or helping to facilitate their growth where they have declined, as a protective and preventive strategy. Community practice therefore is *par excellence* the optimum intervention strategy for promoting social inclusion, preventing harm and by extension safeguarding children. It does not as is sometimes assumed, exclude work with individuals. The spectrum of activity includes (Smale et al., 2000; Wright, 2004):

- **Direct intervention:** work carried out with individuals, families and local networks to tackle problems that directly affect them.
- **Indirect Intervention:** work with community groups and other professionals and agencies to tackle problems affecting a range of people.
- **Change agent activity:** this seeks to change ways that people relate to each other that are responsible for social problems whether at individual, family or neighbourhood levels by reallocating resources.
- **Service delivery activity:** providing services that help to maintain people in their own homes, to reduce risks to vulnerable children and young people, and provide relief to parents and carers.

Community practice is not just about transforming neighbourhoods whether on a small or large scale but it can also enable personal change and growth in individuals through social action and the fostering of co-operative activity. The reverse of course is also true. Individual work such as that described earlier in this book that focuses on the internal problems of children and families can also contribute to wider social transformation in neighbourhoods. Evidence from the Sure Start initiative, although not definitive, does indicate positive effect on family welfare. Defining precisely what community work is can be difficult, it can mean almost what anyone wants it to mean from visiting isolated families to organising a protest march to the Town Hall to lobby for improvements to neighbourhood services (Thompson, 2002; Adams et al., 2000).

You may feel that community practice lacks a focus for your aspiration to facilitate neighbourhood development and empowering experiences for socially excluded people. Groupwork offers the optimum intervention in these circumstances whereby you, together with other staff, can engage in the extension of networks of carers, promotion of self-directed groups and the creation of new resources. Parent support groups can help lonely, vulnerable parents discover mutual support and help build confidence as a vital step towards safer child care practices. Groupwork skills are distinctive but enshrine the core psycho-social base of good practice and can incorporate elements of your existing intervention skills in a preventive format.

Your decision to embark on a groupwork intervention as part of community practice should be on the basis that it is the best way of helping those people concerned, rather than because you want to try it or that it is cheaper than seeing people individually. In the context of safeguarding children and young people being everybody's business groupwork has enormous potential for contributing to the creation of safer neighbourhoods and reducing social isolation which can reduce the risk of child abuse. Groups offer the opportunity to:

- Learn and test interpersonal skills.
- Provide a sense of belonging.
- Empower service users pressing for social change.
- Develop mutual support mechanisms.
- Exchange information and share experiences.

Activity 8.1

Consider the role of your agency in empowerment and socially inclusive practice. Do you recognise practices consistent with that role? List three changes to your practice that aspire to empower service users.

Cultural competence

The concept of cultural competence has begun to emerge in the social science literature as a way of highlighting specific elements of a socially inclusive practice that can improve safeguarding practice. Drawing together the elements of practice that can contribute towards a model of culturally competent care means it is possible to define cultural competence as a set of knowledge-based and interpersonal skills that allow individuals to understand, appreciate and work with individuals of cultures, from other than their own. Five components have been identified (Kim, 1995) comprising culturally competent care:

- Awareness and acceptance of cultural differences.
- Capacity for cultural self-awareness.
- Understanding the dynamics of difference.
- Developing basic knowledge about the child's culture.
- Adapting practice skills to fit the cultural context of the child and family.

These are consistent with other work which critique the historical development of cross-cultural services and offer a model of service organisation and development designed to meet the needs of black and ethnic minority families (Moffic and Kinzie, 1996; Bhugra, 1999; Bhugra and Bahl, 1999). Ethnocentric and particularly Eurocentric explanations of emotional and psychosocial development are not inclusive enough to understand the development of diverse ethnic minority groups. Failure to understand the cultural background of service users can lead to unhelpful child protection assessments, non-compliance, poor use of services, and alienation of the individual or family from the welfare system.

Cultural competence can initially be understood in the context of a desire to improve our practice in order to meet the needs of the growing multi-cultural and ethnically diverse society developing around us. It assumes that historical and orthodox assumptions about human growth and behaviour have served their purpose in meeting the needs of troubled children and young people in particular circumstances and at particular points in time. Now in the early stages of the 21st century changes we are required to address and respond to a modern generation of families and offspring who cannot be easily fitted into existing theoretical paradigms and require safeguarding. There is increasing evidence for the need to refine and develop our methods and models of assessment and intervention so that they are more relevant and accessible to children and young people from a much wider range of backgrounds than was the case in the not too distant past (Madge, 2001).

This is not to say that children and young people in the majority ethnic communities do not require improved methods of help and support. They are being socialised and exposed to a quite different society than former generations. The pace of life, enhanced stressors, individualism, and consumerism are blamed for producing heightened states of arousal and stimulation. Evidence has begun to emerge of genetic changes, the development of new illnesses and of course a range of new risk factors to their mental health – especially the availability of cheap psychoactive drugs and greater access to alcohol. The internet is a source of fascination but also danger as paedophiles use it as a vehicle for grooming vulnerable children. Depictions of family life, for example in children's literature has changed dramatically in the past 40 years from misleading idyllic paternalistic havens of safety and security to the grim reality of poverty, child abuse, divorce, mentally ill parents and personal and institutional racism (Tucker and Gamble, 2001).

Ethnicity requires some clarification as another term that can be used in a variety of contexts but without much thought as to its meaning. Its use alongside the term culture causes confusion especially when the two become almost synonymous. This is because there is no easy definition, but we at least need to know the complexities of the use of the term ethnicity because it perhaps reflects something deeper and more ambivalent about the way we internally manage difference and other-ness. Part of the problem lies in mixing up birthplace with ethnic identity. A white person born in Africa and a black person born in Britain can be defined by their ethnic grouping and place of birth. Further confusion has historically prevailed due to the way the official census data have been collated. In the UK since 1951 the methods of data collection have altered from just recording the country of birth, to the birthplace of parents, to 1981 when there was no question on ethnicity. In 1991 a question on ethnicity offered a range of categories and in 2001 there were further changes to account for citizens with dual or mixed heritage.

The term 'race' is now generally accepted to be redundant as a meaningful scientific category however *the idea of race* as a general descriptor of assumed national, cultural or physical difference persists in society (Amin, 1997). The concept is embraced at the policy level with legislation such as the Race Relations Act in the UK and institutions such as the Commission for Racial Equality. Legislation such as the 1989 Children Act, the 2004 Children Act and 2004 Children's National Service Framework which contextualise work with children and young people, expects practitioners to take account of a child's religious persuasion, racial origin, and cultural and linguistic background, without adequate guidance as to what is meant by 'race' or 'culture'. The issue becomes more complex when we consider census data that show the increase in numbers of children from dual and mixed heritage backgrounds and consider the particularly complex set of problems they can encounter (Walker, 2005).

Applying theory to practice

In the context of integrated practice, multidisciplinary and interprofessional working there is an opportunity to maximise the effectiveness of interventions to meet the diverse needs of multi-cultural societies and service users (Magrab et al., 1997; Oberhuemer, 1998;Tucker et al., 1999). The characteristics of such work apply in a framework familiar to all professionals. It begins with assessment then proceeds through decision-making, planning, monitoring, evaluation, and finally to closure. It is argued that this common framework offers the optimum model for encouraging reflective practice to be at the core of contemporary practice (Taylor and White, 2000; Walker, 2002). Reflective practice offers the opportunity to shift beyond functional analysis to making active links between the value base, policy-making process, and the variety of interventions conducted.

Combining reflective practice with culturally competent practice means that you have the opportunity to make a major contribution towards responding to the social policy aspiration of inclusion and anti-oppressive practice. In so doing you can facilitate closer co-operation between professionals engaged in safeguarding children and young people on a shared agenda of challenging institutional and personal discrimination (Eber et al., 1996; VanDenBerg and Grealish; 1996, Sutton, 2000). One of the defining features of contemporary practice is the ability to work closely with other professionals and communities, sometimes in a co-ordinating role or as a client advocate. This role in the context of safeguarding children is crucial at various points of the assessment and intervention process to ensure culturally competent practice.

Issues of citizenship, nationality, race and immigration provide the overarching context within legislation and public policy which sets the scene for racist and oppressive practice to go unchecked and the needs of black children to be overlooked. In the United Kingdom, the **British Nationality Act 1948** provided legal rights to immigration which have served as a focal point for a continuing racialised debate about the numbers of black immigrants and refugee/asylum seekers and the perceived social problems subsequently caused (Solomos, 1989). The **Race Relations (Amendment) Act 2000** came into force in 2001 extending the scope of the **Race Relations Act 1976** to counter racism. The new Act strengthens the law in two ways that are significant to child protection practice:

- It extends protection against racial discrimination by all public authorities, making the legislative remit wider by covering any service provided to the public.
- It places a new, enforceable positive duty on public authorities to not just avoid racial discrimination, but to actively promote better race relations in the community.

The **Nationality, Immigration and Asylum Act 2002** is the fourth piece of primary legislation attempting to reform the asylum system in 10 years. Previous measures related to dispersal and support measures and were widely regarded as harmful to children because they resulted in sub-standard accommodation, isolation, discrimination and poverty (Dennis and Smith, 2002; JCWI, 2002). The new law proposes establishing accommodation centres housing huge numbers of people in rural areas. Protection of children in such places is difficult due to the high turnover of residents, while these children and young people are impeded from opportunities to integrate and feel part of society.

In addition, the new law denies asylum-seeking children the right to be educated in mainstream local schools. Such segregation contravenes the **Human Rights Act 1998** and the UN Convention on the Rights of the Child (1989) because this is not in the best interests of the child and will very likely harm their development and mental health. Children, who have suffered extreme trauma, abuse, anxiety and hardship, need to feel safe, included and part of their community with their peers in order to begin to thrive and rebuild their fragile sense of self.

Socially excluded groups

Inspection of services for black children and their families in Britain shows that despite years of rhetoric of anti-racist and anti-oppressive social work practice, assessments and care planning are still generally inadequate (SSI, 2002). The guidance suggests:

- Ensuring that services and staffing are monitored by ethnicity to ensure they are provided appropriately and equally.
- Involving ethnic minorities in planning and reviewing services.
- Training in anti-racist and anti-discriminatory practice.
- Investigating and monitoring complaints of racial discrimination or harassment.
- Explicit policies are in place for working with black families.

Skills in facilitating service user empowerment are indicated in any vision of the future shape of service provision (Walker, 2001c). A psycho-social practice framework employing community work and groupwork skills are also required to enable black families and young people to support each other and raise collective awareness of shared issues. Investigation of indigenous healing practices and beliefs provide a rich source of information to utilize in the helping process. Advocacy skills in which young people are encouraged to be supported and represented by advocates of their choice with a children's rights perspective, would help contribute to influencing current service provision (Ramon, 1999). A traditional psycho-social practice, that links the internal and external world of the client, augmented with culturally competent skills, can help meet the needs of socially excluded children and families.

Continual reflection and evaluation of practice is required to maintain an anti-racist socially inclusive practice. Recognising racial harassment as a child protection issue and as an indicator for subsequent potential mental health problems is evidence for example, of how you can translate policy generalisation into specific practice change. Workers who make sure they take full account of a child's religion, racial, cultural and linguistic background in the decision making process are demonstrating the link between social policy and socially inclusive practice. Ensuring for example, that black children in residential care have access to advocates and positive role models can assist in challenging institutionally racist practice. Anti racist and anti-oppressive practice will help develop strategies to overcome value judgements about the superiority of white British family culture and norms.

Activity 8.2

What could you do personally to translate policy guidance into effective practice with black and ethnic minority families?

Commentary

Continual reflection and evaluation of your practice will enable you to maintain an anti-racist practice. Recognising racial harassment as a child protection issue is crucial and making sure you take full account of a child's religion, racial, cultural and linguistic background in the decision making process. In some schools racist bullying does occur often in subtle ways. Developing strategies to overcome value judgements about the superiority of white British family culture and norms requires continual checking of your assumptions about family life.

You need to explore the impact of white power and privileges in your relationships with black people and draw connections between racism and the social control elements of professional practice. Rejecting stereotypes of black and ethnic minority family structures and relationships will enable you to assess the rich diversity of families and permit the building of an assessment not based on a deficit model judged against an Anglo centric norm. The more powerlessness is reinforced by services which deny felt experience and choice, and practitioners expect partnership without addressing the impact of powerlessness, the less users will be empowered (Braye and Preston-Shoot, 1995).

Disabled children

There are a growing number of disabled children and young people living in the community who are socially excluded, subject to abuse and needing high levels of support. About 394,000 children under

16 in Britain are disabled with more than 100,000 severely disabled (DoH, 2000a). Recent research has highlighted the under-reporting of the abuse of disabled children (Morris, 1998). *The Common Core of Skills and Knowledge for The Children's Workforce* (DfES, 2005a) states that everyone working with disabled children should:

- Be able to recognise the signs of possible developmental delay.
- Be able to support children and young people with a developmental difficulty or disability.
- Understand that their families, parents and carers will also need support and reassurance.
- Know and recognise that for some children and young people delayed or disordered development may stem from an underlying, potentially undiagnosed disability and not a reflection of parenting skills.

This is important given the emphasis in *Every Child Matters* on the link between poor parenting and poor outcomes which is being misinterpreted as blaming children's behavioural problems on parents. For children with autism including Asperger's syndrome which are complex and generally under-diagnosed, the risk is that their needs may go unmet leading to school exclusion and putting them at risk of abuse or neglect.

A social model of disability rather than an impairment-specific model, can be useful in recognising the environmental barriers to disabled children that prevent them participating equally in society and thus promoting their protection from abuse. This model emphasises the need to identify the way in which structures and institutions further disable people with disabilities so that these can be challenged (Sharkey, 2000).

Children with a severe disability want to know how to deal with the social and psychological challenges they face – including dealing with other family members, coping with their own negative feelings, and planning for the future. It is important to recognise that disabled children who are abused probably find it harder to disclose due to a mixture of their disabilities and the inability of professionals to recognise the signs. Families require relief and a range of support including home-based sitting services, residential or family-based respite care, or long-term care from social services departments that decreases risks to the children (Beresford et al., 1996).

Lone parents with disabled children, families from ethnic minorities, and families caring for the most severely disabled children have the highest levels of unmet need, and live in the poorest conditions. The mental health needs of disabled children are often masked by a narrow focus on their disability through a medical, rather than social model of disability. Behaviour causing concern can often be ascribed to the physical or intellectual disability rather than a separate psychological need. Signs and symptoms of abuse can be reasoned away by other explanations. Thoughtful assessment in these circumstances is crucial.

The Disability Discrimination Act 1995 (Part 3) requires that social services and other service providers must not discriminate against disabled children by refusing to provide any service which is provided to other children, by providing a lower standard of service or offering a service on less favourable terms. The needs of deaf children like other disabled children are often overlooked or simply poorly understood. The medical model of disability ensures that the disability itself is the focus of attention rather than the disabling environment and attitudes of society. Very little research has been undertaken with this particularly socially excluded group to try to understand their emotional and psychological needs and the impact on them of their disability. Deaf culture needs to be taken into account if a socially inclusive practice is to be employed. Its principle characteristics are:

- Sharing a common language (BSL) for communication purposes.
- Social interaction choices.
- Identity issues.
- Historic understanding of discrimination.

The low uptake of respite services by Asian parents with a disabled child are still perceived by some as evidence of the closed network of familial relationships within Asian culture, rather than evidence of the inaccessibility of existing service provision. Sometimes this is a matter of proper translating services being unavailable but it can also represent a lack of effort from social workers and other social care professionals to understand the families they aspire to help. For example, some Asian families are reluctant to have daughters cared for by male carers, or they simply have little knowledge of the health and welfare system in Britain (Shah, 1992). Even when good translators are available they do not always manage to convey the subtleties of meaning related to feelings and cultural differences. Trying to distinguish the needs of children and young people with a physical or learning disability is difficult enough for many professionals let alone for Black families already disadvantaged and discriminated against.

Activity 8.3

In what ways do you think that the safeguarding guidance does not achieve its aims in relation to helping you meet the needs of disabled children and their families?

Commentary

The Carers and Disabled Children Act 2000 entitles all carers, including parent carers, to be assessed in their own right. But assessments and eligibility criteria seem to be less of a problem than a shortage of services to meet assessed needs. A lack of flexibility within social services provision often means families having to adjust to fit whatever services are available – rather than services fitting their needs. The Children Act 1989 mirrors many of the provisions in the UN Convention on the Rights of the Child ostensibly promoting social inclusion. However local authorities have continued to locate the issue of exclusion within the disabled child rather than in the *external social and environmental factors contributing to exclusion*. This results in social services departments attempting to meet their obligations by locating care outside the disabled child's home, away from their families, and in ways that remove them from their communities (Morris, 1998).

Young offenders

According to recent figures there were 11,500 young people aged 15 to 20 in jail in England and Wales in 2000, of those 90 per cent had a diagnosable mental health disorder, histories of child abuse and many had substance abuse problems as well as personality disorders (Lyon et al., 2000). Young offenders are among the most socially excluded groups in society and the evidence suggests that imprisonment simply makes matters worse not better. Within two years of release, 75 per cent will have been reconvicted and 47 per cent will be back in jail (Social Exclusion Unit, 2002). If some of these young people become homeless or end up in insecure accommodation, they are between eight and 11 times more likely to develop mental health problems (Stephens, 2002).

Young offenders are three times as likely to have a mental health problem due to childhood abuse as other young people. Yet these problems are often neglected because there are no proper methods for screening and assessing mental health problems within the youth justice system (Farrington, 1996; Goodman and Scott, 1997; Royal College of Psychiatrists, 2002; Mental Health Foundation, 2002). Your assessment and intervention practice can make a huge difference to this vulnerable group of young people by:

- Challenging multi-agency decision-making meetings to consider alternatives to custodial sentences.
- Articulating the psychological and mental health needs of young offenders.
- Offering supportive interventions and diversionary activities to at risk young people.
- Combining and networking with like-minded staff from other agencies to offer groupwork or individual counselling to disaffected youth.

Prison is no place for safeguarding young people. The risk of suicide is all too evident with frequent reports of suicide in young offenders' institutions. 190 children have killed themselves in custody in England and Wales since 1990 (Social Exclusion Unit, 2002). Even the most progressive regimes are inadequate to the task of meeting these already damaged individuals' needs for stability, certainty, care, and proper support to tackle their offending behaviour within a context of restorative justice and personal responsibility, backed up by therapeutic input.

Looked after children

Nearly 60,000 children were being looked after by local authorities for the year ending 2002 since when the numbers have been declining. About 60 per cent of these children had been abused or neglected with a further 10 per cent coming from 'dysfunctional families' (DoH, 2001). Abuse of this nature can lead to self-harming behaviour, severe behavioural problems and depression. 38,400 of these children were in foster placements and 6,400 were in children's homes, yet foster carers and residential staff are among the least qualified and supported people left to manage sometimes extreme behaviour.

One in nine children will run away for at least one night before they are 16. Around 100,000 children run away from home or care every year, placing themselves at great risk. Many report being abused as the reason. The **Homelessness Act 2002** extends the safety net to young people leaving state care who are vulnerable to homelessness where they are likely to become involved in crime, drug abuse and exposed to personal danger. The Act places a duty on local authorities to develop strategies to tackle and prevent homelessness. Combined with the **Children (Leaving Care) Act 2000** these measures should enable staff working with young people to intervene to improve the safety and welfare of a highly disadvantaged group.

A recent research study emphasised the importance of a preventive approach with children in the public care system who are more likely to be excluded from school following emotional and behavioural difficulties (Fletcher-Campbell, 2001). Teacher training that fails to adequately prepare newly-qualified staff to respond to the needs of pupils is considered to be a factor in the increased use of school exclusions (OFSTED, 1996). Unless the mental health needs of these children and young people are addressed as part of a strategy that effectively nurtures children's inclusion in school, the risk of deterioration is high.

The new integrated children's system is designed to maximise the opportunity for looked after children to develop and sustain secure attachments which are recognised as fundamental to long term healthy outcomes. There are two public service agreement targets supporting the drive to providing permanent families for children where positive attachments can thrive:

- To increase by 40 per cent the number of looked after children who are adopted.
- To increase to 95 per cent the proportion of looked after children placed for adoption once the decision to adopt has been made.

Refugee and asylum seeking children

Refugee and asylum seekers are among the most disadvantaged ethnic minority group for whom culturally competent practice is essential. Some are unaccompanied, and many are affected by extreme circumstances that might include witnessing the murder of parents or kin, dislocation from school and community and severing of important friendships. Lack of extended family support, loss of home, and prolonged insecurity add to their sense of vulnerability. These experiences can trigger symptoms of post traumatic stress syndrome, a variety of mental health problems and increase their vulnerability to abuse (Dwivedi, 2002).

Parents' coping strategies, ability to protect their children and overall resilience can be diminished in these trying circumstances. The self-regulatory patterns of comfort and family support usually available at times of stress can be disrupted. Your involvement needs to take a broad holistic and psycho-social approach to intervention and not overlook the need for careful assessment of mental health problems developing in adults and children, whilst responding to practical demands. If these are not tackled promptly these people may go on to develop serious and persistent difficulties which are harder, and more costly to resolve, in the long term.

The number of applications for asylum from unaccompanied under 18s almost trebled between 1997 and 2001 from 1,105 to 3,469. DoH figures indicate that there were 6,750 unaccompanied asylum-seeking children supported by local authorities in 2001. Further evidence shows that many of these young people were accommodated and receiving a worse service than other children in need (Audit Commission, 2000). A recent report by the Chief Inspector of Prisons (2004) found that child protection policies are inadequate in all the short term holding centres for asylum seeking families.

Gay, lesbian and bi-sexual young people

An example of the importance of having a supportive adult is provided when we reflect on the way homosexuality is perceived by children and young people. Evidence suggests that young people feel socially excluded in a culture where heterosexuality is portrayed as the norm and any inquisitiveness or ambiguity ruthlessly denigrated. This is an area about which little research has been undertaken and is the subject of lively discussion and prescriptive policy from governments. In the context of rising levels of suicide among young males and the burgeoning literature on the widely reported crisis of identity among young men apparently usurped by years of feminist critiques of patriarchal society and gender abuse of power, we need to understand how children and young people construct and internalise concepts of gender (Laufer, 1985). The invisibility of lesbian and gay role models or thoughtful discussion in social contexts conspire to construct a sense of danger and shame as adolescents experiment and explore different aspects of their sexuality.

A study recently explored the use of homophobic terms by boys and young men and the meanings invoked when they use them, in order to find evidence that might help explain masculinity and adult sexual identity formation in later years (Plummer, 2001). The study found that homophobic terms come into currency in primary school but usually with little connection with sexual connotations. Interestingly, this early use of homophobic terms such as 'poofter' and 'faggot' occurs prior to puberty, prior to adult sexual identity formation and prior to knowing much at all about homosexuality. The effect seems to be that early homophobic experiences provide an important reference point for boys and young men comprehending forthcoming sexual identity formation.

Young carers

There are many thousands of children and young people who are caring for sick or disabled relatives across Britain. In the 2001 census about 175,000 young people were identified as providing unpaid care in their families. The Carers National Association defines a young carer as:

> . . anyone under the age of 18 whose life is in someway restricted because of the need to take responsibility for the care of a person who is ill, has a disability, is experiencing mental distress or is affected by substance use or HIV/Aids.

Their needs have been systematically neglected by education, health and social care agencies for too long. This is an area where inter-agency communication is crucial, especially between adult and children's services since staff from both may be supporting different members of the same household. There is a concern that the creation of new integrated children's services may risk less effective collaboration between these adult and children's workers.

Most young carers (63 per cent) care for people with physical health problems, while 29 per cent care for people with mental health problems. Fourteen per cent care for people with learning disabilities and this is likely to include caring for a sibling with a learning disability. Four per cent care for a person with a sensory disability. Recent research indicates the impact these caring responsibilities have on their welfare (CAN, 2003):

- Reduced educational and future career prospects.
- Victims of bullying.
- Health problems, including physical harm and mental health difficulties.
- Low income, poor housing and poverty.
- 3,700 young carers looked after due to parents' disability.

Elements of socially inclusive practice

Critics suggest that reorganising children's services as a means to improving inter-agency co-operation, will not succeed because professional groups tend to create their own boundaries irrespective of organisational structure (Reder and Duncan, 2003). Also there is strong evidence that it is the organisational *climate* rather than the structure that is a major predictor of improved outcomes in children's services (Glisson and Hemmelgarn, 1998).

Practitioners have to assess needs, evaluate risks and allocate resources in a way that is equitable as far as possible for children and young people in child protection situations. Challenging oppression in relation to key issues such as poverty and social marginalisation that underpin interactions in social welfare requires a holistic approach to social change that tackles oppression at the personal, institutional and cultural levels (Dominelli, 2002). An empowering practice can contribute to the defence of marginalised people and better safeguard children.

Anti-racist and anti-oppressive practice are repeatedly referred to in the professional literature in health, education and social work and have a long historical lineage as part of the social justice basis of modern practice. The concepts are backed up in codes of conduct, ethical guidance and occupational standards requiring services to meet the needs of diverse cultures and combat discrimination. They are part and parcel of what attracts many into vocational work in the first place. Translating good intentions is however harder than it might at first appear.

For example in the case of child care practice there is still a tendency for staff to proceed with assessment on the basis that the mother is the main responsible carer with the father taking a minor role. Women are perceived therefore as responsible for any problems with their children and for their protection. You may feel that this reflects the reality especially in cases of single parenthood, or domestic violence where fathers are absent or a threat. Anti-oppressive practice requires in these situations acknowledgement of the mother's predicament and multiple dilemmas for example when women decline to press charges against abusive partners fearing retribution. It requires an informed practice using feminist theory to appreciate the patriarchal power structures in society, evaluate the situation, and seek every small opportunity to support the mother and engage the father.

The characteristics of non-Western societies such as collectivism, community and physical explanations for emotional problems are in harmony with a socially inclusive perspective but are in contrast to Western concepts of individualism and psychological explanations (Bochner, 1994). The Western model of mental illness ignores the religious or spiritual aspects of the culture in which it is based. However, Eastern, African and Native American cultures tend to integrate them (Fernando, 2002). The significance of adult mental health problems as a risk factor in child protection is well established and has led to criticisms of the lack of integrated practice between adult mental health and child protection services.

Spirituality and religion do not feature often in the child protection literature, yet they can be critical components of a young person's well being, offering a source of strength and hope in trying circumstances. You need to address this dimension as part of the constellation of factors affecting families where this features, avoiding stereotyping, and bearing in mind the positive and sometimes negative impact spiritual or religious beliefs might have on children's safety. Black and other ethnic minority families where strong religious beliefs are held require particular sensitivity where their faith and cultural practices do not correspond to Eurocentric models. Basing your practice on anti-oppressive principles is not a soft option, signing up to political correctness, or about being nice to black people. It is about how you define yourself as a worker and your relationship to children and young people.

A recent powerful contribution to the literature on this issue makes the point that you cannot bolt-on a bit of anti-oppressive practice, it has to be part and parcel of all your everyday practice as a contribution to tackling poverty, social justice, and the structural causes of inequality (Dominelli 2002). This means articulating an anti-racist, socially inclusive agenda in every possible context and challenging attempts to deny or avoid the issue. Equally it especially does not imply that when working with a black family you should not challenge parents or carers who deny access or avoid contact where concerns have been raised about child safety.

Care, control and partnership

This tension between care and control and the ambiguity from which it arises is apparent in government guidance, for example partnership practice figures prominently elsewhere, yet it is not emphasised in the elements on risk with their greater stress on protection and control. This points to the apparent conflict between an emphasis on working in partnership with service users – which is fundamental to modern practice – and the statutory requirement to protect vulnerable children (Jack and Walker, 2000).

Whilst the values underpinning partnership practice and the evidence of its efficacy are fairly unequivocal, this is not the case with the requirement to protect and control where there is much greater ambiguity about both the values on which it is based and the practice methods which it involves. The problem of the social and cultural relativism of concepts of dangerousness and significant harm create uncertainty for practitioners. Similar problems exist in relation to the values underpinning practice in relation to control and protection.

Thus both the underpinning values and methods associated with practice in relation to control and protection are fraught with uncertainty and seem far removed from the aspirations of partnership. It is important to acknowledge these tensions and recognise that a defining characteristic of good assessment practice is the need to balance these competing demands within different forms of practice. These try to maintain your commitment to the value base of professionalism whilst fulfilling your duty to both care and control.

Partnership practice

For children and young people participation needs to be appropriate to its context and to take account of the issues involved, the objectives sought and the young people who make up the target group. Different kinds of participation might be appropriate for different parts of a safeguarding project or at different stages in a child protection investigation. The following barriers and solutions to the participation of children and young people in social care service development and strategic planning in general were identified in recent research (McNeish and Newman, 2002):

Barriers

- **Attitudes:** many children think nothing happens as a result of their involvement and are less willing to get involved.
- **Time:** proper consultation and involvement take time.
- **Methods:** children find formality, complexity and bureaucracy off putting. *Forums* are the least favourite methods, although local authorities commonly use these.
- **Lack of information:** many children don't hear about chances to get involved; there is often little feedback about what has happened as a result.

Solutions

- **Support mechanisms:** adults need to support children in decision-making, thinking carefully about how and when to intervene. Staff need support to change their way of working, to be given time to involve children and to increase their skills in talking and listening to children.
- **Methods children like:** variety is needed; so is fun. Groups are popular; children tend to like talking rather than writing and to talk in groups rather than one to one.

Little is currently known about why young people choose not to be involved or why they get excluded. There is a research gap about issues to be addressed when trying to involve excluded children and young people in participation. It is recommended that the notion of being 'hard to reach' is examined, as there is a danger in seeing this as something to do with the young people rather than a reflection on the agency's ability to communicate with a diverse group. It appears that the voices of younger children, disabled children (particularly those with communication or learning difficulties) and children and young people from black and ethnic minority backgrounds (who may have English as a second language) or from families living in poverty can remain unheard. This reinforces the importance of developing children's services staff skills in direct work with children.

There is a lack of research, monitoring and evaluation on the impact and outcomes of the participation of children and young people on change and improvement in child protection services. There is some knowledge about participation techniques but little or no examination of the relationship between the process and the achievement of tangible change. It is reported that children and young people can gain personally from positive experiences of participation. Feeding back the results of their participation to children and young people is vital as it is related to engagement and commitment. It is recommended that some knowledge-based standards could be developed (with children and young people) around evaluating participation impact, tracking change and feeding back to participants.

It is also worth noting that there is much that is helpful to learn about children's participation from participation developments with adult service users. Children's involvement would be supported by developing an explicitly participatory approach to practice with training developed to enable this to happen, including imaginative approaches to training involving the viewpoints and involvement of children and young people. Partnership practice whilst apparently being at odds with some of the requirements of child protection work is in fact one of the methods through which this balance can be sought – if not always attained. The next activity is intended to clarify this.

Activity 8.4

Write a paragraph describing how you think working in partnership with service users can help to integrate the requirements of both care and control. In doing this you might find it helpful to briefly re-read the section on the social construction of risk in Chapter 5 (page 73).

Commentary

In the section on social construction we discussed the social and cultural factors involved in the definition and perception of dangerousness. Working in partnership involves a genuine commitment to the attempt to understand the world from the client's perspective and communicating this effectively without necessarily condoning any particular behavioural expression of their perception of the world. Partnership however also involves mutuality – there is an expectation that the client will be willing to make a similar attempt to understand the perceptions and behaviours of others. Obviously the worker has the professional responsibility to enable clients to work on problems in this way when initially the nature of their problems may inhibit the flexibility which this entails. This will involve entering the social and cultural context of the client – rather than attempting to promote change by imposing an alien cultural context.

In such ways partnership practice can work with the social and cultural relativity which, as we have seen, is a characteristic of assessment practice. What may be seen as the problem of ambiguity and uncertainty which in some circumstances leads to draconian attempts to control, can in this way be turned into a positive strength in the attempt to care and enable. In this case, knowledge of cultural diversity, the skills of interpretation and negotiation in building partnership, and the values of individualisation and respect for uniqueness and diversity are the foundation of such partnership practice. It is important to acknowledge that the commitment to partnership should not be misinterpreted as an invitation to relinquish boundaries in professional relationships. Loss of boundaries can place vulnerable children and workers at risk.

Key Chapter Points

- Social disadvantage, unemployment, bad housing and impoverished surroundings are among the characteristics of socially excluded families and indicate risk factors for child abuse. However, poverty does not cause child abuse.

- There is increasing evidence for the need to refine and develop our methods and models of assessment and intervention so that they are more relevant and accessible to children and young people from a much wider range of backgrounds, cultures and ethnic communities.

- A traditional psycho-social practice, that links the internal and external world of the client, augmented with culturally competent skills, can help meet the needs of socially excluded children and families.

- Challenging oppression in relation to key issues such as poverty and social marginalisation that underpin interactions in social welfare requires a holistic approach to social change that tackles oppression at the personal, institutional and cultural levels.

- Spirituality and Religion do not feature often in the child protection literature, yet they can be critical components of a young person's well being, offering a source of strength and hope in trying circumstances.

- Knowledge of cultural diversity, the skills of interpretation and negotiation in building partnership, and the values of individualisation and respect for uniqueness and diversity are the foundation of partnership practice.

Chapter 9

Reviewing and Ending Safely

Learning Objectives

- Demonstrate the importance and purpose of a child care review.
- Understand the significance of enabling children and young people to express their views.
- Ensure that transfer of cases happens speedily with maximum inter-agency communication.
- Describe the importance of reflective practice and supervision.

Reviews and endings in activity designed to safeguard children and young people are among the pivotal points in the process of child protection work. They need to be approached and understood with considerable thought, reflection and creativity. Decisions made at review conferences such as de-registration, closure or the commencement of care proceedings are just as critical as the decisions made at initial meetings and conferences at the beginning of contact. Reviewing and ending your work is an opportunity to take stock of situations in which considerable anxiety may have been exercised during fast-moving events over a short, intense period of time. Or this process could be undertaken regularly at pre-planned punctuations during a period of sustained intervention and activity over a longer course of time. Evidence suggests that in contrast to the large volume of research that has identified the varied consequences of child abuse and investigations into deaths of children who were known to helping agencies, there is little research that has examined effective processes and outcomes of interventions.

Knowing what works is as important as what went wrong in child protection activity, and one of the most overlooked sources for this information is parents themselves. Dale (2004) investigated several recent studies and concluded that:

- **There is a strong tendency for parents to be highly critical of the processes and outcomes of child protection interventions.**
- **Parental perceptions offer insightful contributions that can help improve good child protection practice.**

This is important because it underlines the importance of establishing partnership practice even with hostile parents who resent your involvement. The evidence suggests that parents will respond to staff perceived as friendly, interested, concerned and keen to help. Equally they feel reluctant to engage with help when staff are perceived to be patronising, provocative and punitive. Child abuse arouses very strong emotions in staff who work with children and young people. It is quite natural to feel anger, rage, hate and violent emotions when encountering abusive or neglectful parents. These feelings need to be recognised, understood and managed so that they do not impede the establishment of a positive working relationship. It is this relationship which more than anything, will help safeguard a child or young person, as much as following agency procedures.

This chapter will help your work with families to safeguard children and young people and your understanding of the importance of reviewing and ending intervention in ways that are safe and effective. It will provide evidence of good practice that enables practitioners and parents to appreciate each other's perspective and move forward to safeguard children. The process of ending child protection intervention is described and analysed using research evidence to identify best practice. The movement of families from one area to another is highlighted as a particularly risky time when communication, information exchange and inter-agency collaboration are critical.

What is a review?

Reviews are everybody's business. They are not the responsibility of a particular child protection professional or agency. And they should involve children and parents as much as possible consistent with the particular circumstances and needs of the child as emphasised in The Children Act 1989, the Human Rights Act 1998 and the Children Act 2004. Reviews should not be considered unusual or convened in haste in order to allocate blame when something goes wrong. They should be regarded as routine – and no less important than any other part of the child protection process. Reviews must relate and link explicitly to the current child protection plan.

The way reviews and endings are thought about will affect the attitudes and behaviour of everyone involved in child protection cases. A review might be thought of as an ending in itself – a way of taking stock and summarising the work to date so that a neat ending can be arrived at. If practitioners feel that way then they may inadvertently close their minds to new information or changed circumstances that suggest further involvement. If on the other hand a review is considered as a staging post in a journey where evidence can be weighed, evaluated and compared against baseline data recorded at the start of an intervention, then it ought to be a temporary punctuation. In the context of safeguarding children a review must examine the existing child protection plan and measure progress – or lack of it, against that. The purpose of the review is to:

- Ensure that action plans, programmes, targets, aims and objectives are being kept to.

- Ensure that work involved is consistent with participants personal expectations in terms of values, ethics, paramount safety of children and commitment to family welfare.

- Examine the child protection plan and assesses whether each person is carrying out their part of it within the agreed timescale.

- Determine whether the intended results of an intervention have occurred according to the identified outcomes.

- Ensure the review complies with agency policy, practices and administrative structures.

- Ensure that best practice guidance, research, National and International legislation is used to inform but not detract from making judgements.

There should be no assumptions about the outcome of a review beforehand and practitioners and parents need to approach them with any prejudices or preferences left behind. Self-fulfilling prophecies do happen and the need to close what might be a messy, unhappy and wearing case riddled with uncertainty and frustration could be powerful. The review itself need not be a formal meeting of several professionals as part of statutory requirements, it could be an informal reflective process undertaken by the worker themselves as part of their own self-management. This could mark the beginning of a subtle process that continues into a semi-formal review with a head teacher, supervisor or senior nurse, for example, in which evaluations and assumptions can be safely tested and examined within a supportive relationship. A review can be more formal in the context of inter-agency meetings or case conferences where written and verbal reports are collated, minutes recorded, and specific decisions and action plans are formulated.

Process versus event

The common theme in each of these review contexts is that they are understood *as part of a process* rather than an event, and that the review must be explicitly related to the plan for the children and the intended outcomes in relation to their needs. Practitioners and parents need to focus sharply on whether actions, services and interventions are having the desired effect. For example a health visitor may be helping a parent improve their interactions with a very young child in order to achieve certain developmental milestones. A teacher and educational psychologist may be working with an older child to improve classroom behaviour. Or a housing official may be attempting to advocate for larger accommodation in order to relieve family stress and enable older children to have more privacy in their own bedrooms.

Activity 9.1

Arrange to meet with a colleague from another agency to discuss a recent review at which you were both present. Consider whether the review fulfilled its purpose and if not what you can both do differently in future. Be honest.

Each practitioner in addition to evaluating their own contribution must consider the impact it is having on other interventions. The review might assume co-ordination and complementarity between interventions but in reality a particular combination might be contradictory. For example an educational welfare officer might be aiming to improve school attendance in order to enable a withdrawn child to improve their social skills and self-esteem. But a child and adolescent psychotherapist might assess this child as phobic and unable in the short term to cope with enforced return to school. This contradiction can be highlighted in a review where agreement on the way forward can be negotiated with amendments made to the current plan. Figure 9.1 below illustrates how the Integrated Children's System can be used to identify specific changes required to the current plan avoiding duplication and divergent tasks:

The circular process of assessment, planning, intervention and review is common to all practitioners but in child protection work, due to a variety of factors, reviews and endings tend to impose an artificial finality on the process. This can be due to the need to cease unwelcome involvement by professionals; make decisions regarding registration/de-registration; reach conclusions regarding risk assessment; or move to reduce delay in placement decisions.

These factors combined with high workloads impose a time scale on contact between families and practitioners that can serve to heighten anxiety, increase pressure and neglect the critically important issues around review and closure that require as much attention as the earlier processes of screening, investigation and assessment. For example research shows (Farmer and Owen, 1995):

Identified child's developmental needs and strengths and difficulties in each domain	How will the child's developmental needs be responded to: actions or services to be taken/ provided	Frequency and length of service: e.g. hours per week	Person/agency responsible	Date service will commence/ commenced	Date service completed (if appropriate)	Planned outcomes: progress to be achieved by next review or other specified date
Child's developmental needs						
Parenting capacity						
Family and environmental factors						

Figure 9.1 Changes required to current child protection plan (as agreed at the review meeting) (DoH, 2002)

- Reviews that highlighted areas of risk previously overlooked often failed to influence senior managers expected to make the necessary decisions.

- Once a pattern of case management had been established it was usually endorsed at subsequent reviews even when it was deficient.

The assumption at many case conferences is that a case closes because a child's name is removed from the child protection register. This is a false and potentially fatal assumption. The focus should always be on the child and their needs. A child is likely to still be defined as a child in need and requiring on-going help. The evidence strongly suggests that de-registration often results in a withdrawal of the very resources maintaining safety and the essential support required by many families.

A combination of worker impatience to close cases and parents desire to avoid scrutiny could jeopardise an opportunity to establish healthy trusting relationships and pave the way for family support intervention that will in the long run better safeguard children's safety. Why is this so? Partly this is a question of resources but it is equally and perhaps more importantly about the way child protection and family support are perceived as separate areas of work rather than seamless parts of a continuous process:

- Reviews should examine the child protection plan and assess whether each person is carrying out their part of it within the agreed timescale.

- Reviews need to determine whether the intended results of an intervention have occurred according to the identified outcomes for each service or action in terms of its impact on the child's needs.

- Involving children and families in reviews to the maximum consistent with safety of the child helps foster a sense of respect, feeling valued and maintain effective working relationships.

Activity 9.2

In your next team, staff meeting or professional consultation set aside some time to design ways to involve children and young people in more meaningful ways in reviews about their safety.

Commentary

There is much scope for improved practice in this area according to research evidence and the testimony of children themselves (Jack, 2004). It is important to think from the child or young person's perspective what is going to be helpful rather than implement an abstract general policy. This can lead to tokenism at best and at worst be felt as quite abusive and patronising. You need to spend time explaining what is going on and make sure you are ascertaining the young person's wishes and feelings. For example they may not feel able to attend a review but want to send a representative. They may want to write down their thoughts and feelings or compose a poster illustrating their point of view. Or they may prefer to attend with an advocate who will speak on their behalf. You must be flexible and child-centred in your thinking and actions and mindful of the guilt, mixed feelings and resistance within children at the centre of child protection concerns.

Change and outcomes

Reviews should be seen as part and parcel of the process of change. The review itself aims to establish what if anything has changed in the family of concern. Changes can take place in people's behaviour, perceptions and feelings. The act of reviewing may itself provoke changes – it can serve to motivate families to try harder or plunge them into despair and hopelessness. In other words it is not just an administrative or procedural exercise. It is crucial that everyone understands the feelings and dynamics generated during review and before endings because these can inform their understanding of the work at hand. This applies just as much to families as to workers. Certain feelings may provoke false hope or equally false fears leading to actions that are unsupported by hard evidence. A variety of responses to the prospect of change could be detected – for example a worker and parent or carer might both feel:

- **Relief** at the prospect of some decision being made.
- **Guilt** at the need for a review due to plans failing.
- **Sadness** at the potential for loss.
- **Confusion** at the mixed messages being given.
- **Anxiety** at the negative consequences.
- **Anger** at feeling judged.
- **Happiness** at knowing something is going to happen.
- **Ambivalence** at wanting help but not what is being offered.

Parents often feel abandoned once a child is removed from the child protection register yet this is probably the most important time to continue work to support them and help build those skills necessary to meet their child's developmental needs. It is equally crucial that practitioners in supervisory or conference contexts are aware of the impact powerful feelings are having on their judgement. What do these feelings tell us about the way the family are managing the protection of the children of concern? If there is a great deal of anxiety in the professional system does this mirror the same feelings in the family facing withdrawal of professional involvement? Understanding these complex processes can enable reflection back on the plan and the previously identified needs of the children to see whether change has occurred, to what degree and if it is being sustained.

The issue of de-registration has come to represent an important official indicator of improved child protection, reduction of risk and by implication greater safeguarding of children. However, research demonstrates that in a significant number of cases where de-registration occurred due to a change in the official perception of risk, there was no real improvement in the safety of the child (Peters and Barlow, 2003).

Evidence demonstrates that it is common for the needs of the main carer to be neglected in child protection work (Brandon et al., 1999). Parental needs tend to go unmet when important areas of difficulty are not recognised such as domestic violence, drug and alcohol abuse, the mental health needs of children, or due to the alienation of parents during the investigative child protection process. Where parents' needs are recognised however, children's needs are in danger of being sidelined when the parent is the main focus of intervention. Effective safeguarding of children should aim for both rather than constructing a false and dangerous dichotomy between the two.

This jeopardises future prospects for children's safety especially when the developmental needs of the children go unmet when reviews focus on incidents of abuse rather than taking an ecological and developmental approach. For example there may be an absence of incidents of abuse in a period under review but harm to the child could still be happening in terms of missed developmental milestones, weight loss, poor school attainment, disturbed behaviour or lack of social contact. It is important to consider the wider picture and not rely on a limited range of indicators.

Organisational needs do impact negatively on service delivery in relation to safeguarding children. Workload stress, targets, inspections, unallocated cases, plus unexpected illness or vacancy cover might increase pressure to close a case that parents would prefer to remain open. The review process should identify expected outcomes to the intervention plan that provide concrete measures to evaluate whether an ending is feasible.

Managers in all agencies taking decisions to close cases now have more explicit accountability in child protection work which while leaving the individual worker feeling less vulnerable, should also act as a prompt to ensure that alternative services are put in place. Every person involved needs to consider what part they can play in continuing to focus on meeting the needs of the child. And while the ending may feel abrupt for the family they must ensure that an ending meeting with the family is undertaken in a way that enables and actively encourages them to seek further help if needed. Staff in schools, nurseries, health centres and family centres can be crucial in their support and encouragement of parents at this time. The balance between imposing a support structure and motivating the family to ask for it will be reflected in the degree to which they are reluctant or more enthusiastic about receiving help and support.

Engaging with parents and children

Research suggests that when practitioners work in partnership with parents and children it leads to better outcomes for children (Marsh and Crow, 1998; Calder and Horwath, 1999; Walker, 2001; MacDonald, 2001; Buckley, 2003). The evidence also suggests that practitioners sometimes fail to see children regularly or assume that another worker is doing so (Munro, 2002). It is crucial that children are seen both with their parent and separately. A parents' review of their child's progress should be taken together with other practitioners and your own direct contact with the child.

Children have the right under the terms of the United Nations Convention on the Rights of the Child to be consulted with, and express their views about, services provided for them (UN, 1989). There is a legal duty to do this under the Children Act 1989. Engaging with children in safeguarding contexts will require planning, preparation and creativity. A child already abused or neglected or at risk may be defensive, suspicious and still profoundly loyal to their carer/parent. Time, indirect approaches and the use of age-appropriate materials to nurture conversation will help the process of communication during reviews and endings.

If a child feels too overwhelmed to attend a review their views can be expressed on audio tape or they can be helped to write a letter to the meeting. Practitioners need to be vigilant and sensitive to the child or young person's internal conflict, confusions and split loyalties and treat their opinions cautiously. Parents also need to be aware of their power to influence what their child says. Parents and carers provide over 90 per cent of the care of their children. They are the people who will be in most contact with the child or young person at the centre of concern. When actively involved in reviews parents will respond.

Parents must be seen as partners in the review and with whom an appropriate alliance can be formed, even in the face of profound disagreements about the way forward. There is a legal obligation to involve parents under the Children Act 1989 which may apply even though the child is not looked after because government guidance creates reasonable expectation of discussion and importantly, because of the European Convention of Human Rights expectation that parents must be involved in decision making unless to do so would jeopardise the child's rights to safety or privacy. The notion of partnership and family support challenges assumptions about power, responsibility and ownership, resulting in ambiguity from many staff. Effective partnerships are those based on mutually agreed outcomes and which support endings ensuring that families feel encouraged to approach helping agencies again.

Activity 9.3

Reflect on the above material and draw up a list of the skills and resources you personally need to improve to enable you to maintain a focus on the safety of the child as well as insight into the feelings of parents during reviews

---

Commentary

Reviews are the ideal time to engage in reflective practice. They are an opportunity to think collectively with other practitioners and individually with parents to consider whether a plan is working in the best interests of the child and if not what needs to be changed to better meet their needs. One way of achieving this is in reflective practice. This consists of reflection *in action* or thinking while doing, and reflection *on action* which occurs after an incident takes place. Reflective practice therefore encompasses the need for a useful outcome to the reflective process that will lead to a change in practice. Your list of skills and resources might range from the psychodynamic through to the procedural. You could have strengths in some areas and be able to acknowledge weaknesses that require support and attention. Gaining access to management guidance, supervision or professional consultation in another agency will help you clarify your thoughts.

Positive endings and future support

How to end interventions in ways that ensure it is supportive and can enable families to seek further help in future.

The strong feelings aroused during the process of ending whether it is abrupt or gradually comes to a close, can stop some practical measures being put in place to enable parents and children to seek further help. A follow-up meeting in a few weeks time can act as a vital safeguard during a potentially vulnerable time for the whole family. Telephone numbers of all the agencies involved (day time and night hours) can be provided on a card that can fit into a purse or wallet. A child can be taught what to do to keep safe in the short term and rehearse making contact with a trusted practitioner or helpline. The important point to get across is that there is no shame in needing support and that the sooner help is provided the sooner it will cease to be required.

Integrating knowledge, skills and values in analysing information and being able to weigh its significance and priority as a basis for effective review and ending is a demanding task. Sound reviewing will happen provided the following elements are delineated:

- **Evidencing** changes in the children's developmental needs and circumstances.
- **Comparing** the recorded information in the plan and the evidence presented at the point of review.
- **Being** critically aware of and taking into account the decision making contexts.
- **Consulting** with everyone involved in the work.
- **Being** clear in your thinking and aware of your emotions.

- **Producing** a well-reasoned explanation for the decision that is consistent with the available information.

Ending intervention and reviewing the decision-making process includes thinking and feeling about the situation being addressed. Practitioners' gut feeling when meeting with some families may be that of fear due to threats of violence or intimidation. Parents too may feel anxious and want to run out of the house or not answer the door. But a moment's reflection can enable both to understand that this is probably exactly what the child is feeling because of their over-identification with them. Knowing how the child is feeling can help interpret behaviour and implement any necessary changes to the plan.

Parents achieving even small successes need to be appropriately praised. Teachers can make sure that a child's return to school is noticed and parents praised. Nursery staff need to make positive remarks about the child's care and behaviour to the father or mother when improvements are made. Getting the parent to reflect on how the success happened and ensuring it can be built upon and repeated is essential to keep positive momentum.

Being there when setbacks occur to help and support rather than criticise is crucial. By slowly shifting the focus from monitoring and checking to that of facilitating the parent to measure their own achievements, will set the scene for the withdrawal of the practitioner. Safeguarding children is never a smooth linear process from start to finish. But it is important to avoid drift in practice and cases going on forever. This can lead to lazy practice and families becoming institutionalised. Familiarity can breed contempt on both sides.

At worst this can create the most dangerous life-threatening environment for a child at risk. Practitioners and families need to know what they are aiming to achieve, why they are still receiving attention and when involvement is likely to cease. A decision to disengage or close a case should equally not be taken without supervision, discussion with a line manager and full inter-agency consultation. The factors influencing the decision will include whether the plan is achieving the intended outcomes.

Continuing concerns

What happens when a child moves out of an area if there are continuing concerns but lack of evidence?

Activity 9.4

The case study below gives an example where partnership appears fraught with difficulties and may appear unachievable. You have just been told to review this case and transfer it to another area because the family are moving. Think about how you would try to work in partnership with the family while conveying your concerns to other professionals.

Father (Michael) age 45, unemployed, disabled wheelchair user.
Mother (Susan) age 32, left family 6 months ago, whereabouts unknown.
Daughter (Anne) age 11, at special school for children with learning difficulties
Son (Adam) age 6, attends primary school
Twins (Steve and Linda) age 38 months, Steve is brain damaged and Linda has a hole in her heart. Both have developmental delays.

The family are about to move to another area. The father, Michael, has been uncooperative with many agencies concerned about his children. He has been rude, hostile and racially abusive to black staff. Hospital appointments for the twins have been missed and your concerns have been increasing over time. Adam and Anne bed wet and both have missed a lot of schooling. Father has a history of moving around the country – often at short notice. Michael feels there is nothing much wrong with the children and focuses his attention mostly on the twins. He feels that professionals are exaggerating, he is a proud man and he is determined to care for his family on his own.

Case study commentary

Reflecting on your feelings may produce elements of fear, disapproval, and frustration. Or perhaps you might be aware of a certain admiration for Michael's tenacity and self-sufficiency. You may feel protective towards the children and angry that Michael is not putting their needs first. As a black worker you may want to discuss whether another worker should be allocated this case given his racist language, on the other hand you may feel it is a useful challenge to work with him. You also need to reflect on racist stereotypes of members of the traveller community and consider activating supportive family networks at his intended destination.

Your main anxieties may come from Michael's lack of co-operation and from concerns about the children's developmental needs being neglected. The long-term consequences of this on their personal, educational and social development, together with the impact on Michael of soldiering on heighten your concerns. Michael's anger could be explored to tease out the cause and help him manage it more usefully. Is it due to his wife's exit? Being perceived as an inadequate parent? Professional interference? His feelings of helplessness, and his own needs being eclipsed?

Suggesting a multi-agency case conference between the current and future professional network is useful for planning and using resources and offers a chance to share concerns and measure your level of anxiety against other perspectives. Research shows the absence of case conferences is likely to be detrimental but their occurrence is not always beneficial (Hallett and Birchall, 1995). It will be useful to explore the family's wider network as a possible source of support. Thought also needs to be given to the significance for the children of Susan and her absence. You might think about the use of a contract with Michael. This could set out the purposes of future involvement and what is possible or not in terms of support, help and resources consistent with the child protection plan. It could give Michael space to outline his concerns, need and goals.

A review of the existing plan shows that it is only partly working. These elements are successful:

- Adam and Anne's school attendance has improved slightly.
- The house is cleaner than it used to be.
- Michael has reduced his alcohol use.
- Michael has allowed the health visitor to visit more often.

These elements of the plan have been less successful:

- The twins appointments have not been kept.
- He has refused larger accommodation to enable Anne and Adam to have separate bedrooms.
- Michael often leaves the children with friends when he goes out to the pub in the evening.
- He continues to threaten social workers trying to visit.
- Michael has undermined individual work with Anne and Adam.

As part of the review work, it is crucial to assess whether the developmental needs of each child in the family are being better met. Concerns should be recorded and areas of agreement and disagreement between yourself and Michael and any other professional noted. The review needs to consider whether Michael's moving away is part of a pattern to avoid scrutiny or part of his cultural characteristics or indeed both. It is important to evaluate the strengths in this family as well. Michael is determined to keep the family together. He has some understanding of their needs for schooling and health care. He has acknowledged his alcohol problem. The review may in balancing all the information still decide that Michael cannot be worked with and that legal intervention is the only way to secure the children's welfare.

If this is the case, it is important that such a judgement is soundly based on evidence from other professionals, research, and only comes after all possibilities for engagement have been explored. If Michael moves away quickly before further action can take place agencies at his destination need to be fully informed. Exchange of information and fluent communication is essential. Each separate agency should ensure that their specific part in the protection plan is crystal clear and formally acknowledged at transfer. Responsibility and accountability are now more sharply located with managers. These are the times when vulnerable children may be at most risk because of a combination of disruption in the care network and bureaucratic inertia.

Case closure

The beginning of the end or the end of the beginning?

The criteria for leaving the child protection system are not well defined for worker or family. It is important to understand that leaving the child protection system or removing children's names from the register are not the same as closing a case. Parents may expect no further contact and be confused when told they will still be receiving help. This can provoke feelings of persecution in parents and stress in staff trying to evaluate issues of safety, risk and on-going support. It is critical in these circumstances to maintain the focus on the children's needs. Health visitors for example, are often in the pivotal role of continuing involvement through different phases of child protection and family support intervention.

The evidence from previous child abuse enquiries suggest that it is in cases where the focus on the children's developmental needs has been lost where there is risk of further abuse or death (Hallett and Birchall, 1995). Therefore planning to end contact should commence at the beginning of contact when solid baseline data can be established upon which you and the family can measure progress or lack of it towards clear outcomes. The following questions may be helpful:

- How will the family know that your presence in the family's life has been useful and that the family is better off now than before child protection involvement?

- How will the parents know that the family have reached the point where they feel capable of going on without you?

- How will the family know they have reached the point where they can conduct their own lives without you and the children will be safe?

Such planning needs to be handled especially carefully when dealing with families where child protection concerns are raised but subsequently proved to be unfounded. Getting the balance right is tricky. Openness and clarity should be the hallmark of your involvement but not to the extent where a child's safety may be put at risk. Deciding when and how much information can be shared will depend on fine risk assessment and the judgement of all practitioners involved. Parents will rightly feel upset and angry that they have been excluded to some extent but this should all be planned for in advance.

Careful explanation of the reasons for your actions combined with documentary evidence that any allegations were unfounded are officially recorded will go some way to ease their distress. It is crucial to ensure that the family is not labelled and work is undertaken to rebuild trust so that they feel able to use services open to them in future. However even disproved cases and unfounded suspicions may need to be considered in future intervention because not all disproved cases will necessarily mean children are safe.

The following Figure 9.2 uses the Integrated Children's System to illustrate how a closure record should look so that in the event of transfer to another area the receiving agencies can instantly see where there responsibilities are in terms of the current plan:

Small attainable goals that include solutions rather than an absence of problems help instil feelings of success that can be built upon to achieve outcomes. Nursery staff could show a parent how developmental changes such as increased language skills can be attributed to the parents playing more with the child. A teacher could praise a parent whose child is behaving less disruptively in class as a sign of their improved parenting skills:

- **Endings should be constructive and experienced positively to enable children and families to seek further help when necessary.**

- **The end of child protection concerns should dovetail with continuity of support focused on the child's developmental needs, parental capacity and the wider family environment.**

- **Endings involving families moving to another area must ensure the smooth, speedy exchange of accurate up to date information to every agency concerned, with clear acknowledged action plans.**

Setbacks in child protection plans are normal and should be expected and planned for. Unrealistic goals that fail to be attained undermine confidence and contribute to a spiral of disillusion and discouragement. For example, evidence suggests that parenting classes have high drop-out rates due to staff incompetence and inappropriate referrals therefore it should never be assumed that dropping out means the parent is not committed to change or the protection of their child (NFPI, 2001). Remember that change is hard – especially with long-term entrenched problems.

Reviews and endings are the occasions like beginnings that can set the tone for future contact and activity. Conducted properly, openly and honestly they offer an opportunity for everyone to be clear about their responsibilities and the consequences for not contributing towards their part of the protection plan. Evaluating the plan and drawing reasonable conclusions will depend on everyone's judgement and opinion about the relative importance attached to a variety of factors. A positive factor may be judged to outweigh several negatives and vice versa. Keeping all lines of communication open is crucial – not just when there is agreement but when there is disagreement as well. Families never stand still and positive changes may occur regardless of planned interventions, while negative changes do happen in spite of interventions aimed at helping. Be alert to these events and ready to respond flexibly, creatively and decisively. Never forget how hard being a parent is.

	Child/young persons identified developmental needs, strengths and difficulties	Actions and services provided: both planned and unplanned services and actions	Frequency and length of service: e.g. hours per week	Person/agency responsible	Date services commenced	Planned outcome: progress to be achieved during the course of social services involvement	Date services ended	Actual outcome: progress made, reason services ended or were not provided
Child/young person's health								
Child/young person's education								
Child/young person's emotional and behavioural development								
Child/young person's identity								
Child/young person's family and social relationships								
Child/young person's social presentation								
Child/young person's self-care skills								
Parental capacity								
Family and environmental factors								

Figure 9.2 Summary of interventions and actual outcomes from date of most recent referral

Key Chapter Points

- There should be no assumptions about the outcome of a review beforehand and practitioners and parents need to approach them with any prejudices or preferences left behind. Self-fulfilling prophecies do happen and the need to close what might be a messy, unhappy and wearing case riddled with uncertainty and frustration could be powerful.

- Reviews should be seen as part and parcel of the process of change. The review itself aims to establish what if anything has changed in the family of concern. Changes can take place in people's behaviour, perceptions and feelings. The act of reviewing may itself provoke changes – it can serve to motivate families to try harder or plunge them into despair and hopelessness.

- If a child feels too overwhelmed to attend a review their views can be expressed on audio tape or they can be helped to write a letter to the meeting. Practitioners need to be vigilant and sensitive to the child or young person's internal conflict, confusions and split loyalties and treat their opinions cautiously.

- Reviews are the ideal time to engage in reflective practice. They are an opportunity to think collectively with other practitioners and individually with parents, to consider whether a plan is working in the best interests of the child and if not what needs to be changed to better meet their needs.

- A decision to disengage or close a case should not be taken without supervision, discussion with a line manager and full inter-agency consultation. The factors influencing the decision will include whether the plan is achieving the intended outcomes.

- The evidence from previous child abuse enquiries suggest that it is in cases where the focus on the children's developmental needs has been lost that there is risk of further abuse or death.

- Reviews and endings are the occasions like beginnings that can set the tone for future contact and activity. Conducted properly, openly and honestly they offer an opportunity for everyone to be clear about their responsibilities and the consequences for not contributing towards their part of the protection plan.

Conclusion and Learning Review

Building on your existing skills and knowledge in social care, nursing, youth work or teaching you can make a valuable contribution to the process of assessment and intervention in safeguarding children and young people. The evidence demonstrates that a little help can go a long way especially if that involves enabling other staff, the community, parents or young people themselves to work openly and honestly in creating a more protective environment in which everyone can thrive.

We have examined and reviewed a number of key practical and theoretical resources for practitioners in a variety of contexts in voluntary or statutory agencies who may encounter situations where concerns are expressed about the safeguarding of a child or young person. If your work involves nursing, social work or teaching in the context of child protection, primary care, youth offending, family support, children's nursing, fostering and adoption, youth work, education or probation then this guide has hopefully helped develop your practice. The foundational ideas and practical guidance have been designed to support you in an accessible and sometimes challenging format to create the basis for informed, reflective, confident practice.

This may provide the foundation for you to build a more progressive and advanced knowledge and skills base to continue to improve your child protection practice and expertise in particular areas such as counselling, psychotherapy, or family therapy for example. The guide may also have filled a gap in your learning or reinforced and reaffirmed your practice knowledge and skills to enable you to continue in your work with renewed confidence and energy. If this guide has met your needs then it will have served its purpose or if it has not and requires changes then we would value your feedback and comments in due course. The important thing in a text like this is that it has stimulated your thinking and reflection about the subject and if only in a small way, has made a difference to your practice. Because that difference may make *all the difference* to the child or young person you are working with.

Use this checklist to review your learning having studied this guide. Compare it with your learning profile completed before you began. If there are any areas where it seems your knowledge has not developed sufficiently, revisit the chapters in question, and then, if necessary compare your progress with a colleague, or supervisor. Select some of the suggested further reading in those areas requiring attention. You may in any case want to consider training or further professional development opportunities to continue to develop your practice in this area.

Chapter I: A New Working Environment

I can:	Not at all	Partly	Very well
Describe how changing patterns of service delivery are influencing professional relationships.	○	○	○
Demonstrate understanding of the impact of new legislation, policy and guidance on safeguarding children and young people.	○	○	○

	Not at all	Partly	Very well
Describe the obstacles to, and ways to achieve effective multidisciplinary work.	○	○	○
Understand the principles of integrated working.	○	○	○

Chapter 2: Primary Prevention and Early Intervention

I can:	Not at all	Partly	Very well
Acknowledge the rights of the child and young person across organisations whether survivor or offender.	○	○	○
Achieve an understanding of the family and its place in the community.	○	○	○
Understand the preventative framework required when working with children, young people and their families.	○	○	○
Reflect on individual skills and practices undertaken to promote children's physical, psychological and social well being.	○	○	○

Chapter 3: Children and Young People at Risk

I can:	Not at all	Partly	Very well
Understand modern explanations for child abuse.	○	○	○
Describe risk and resilience factors in children and young people.	○	○	○
Explore and understand the types and causes of abuse.	○	○	○
Identify the signs, symptoms and effects of abuse.	○	○	○

Chapter 4: Collaborative Care

I can:	Not at all	Partly	Very well
Comprehend the necessities of collaborative working across organisations.	○	○	○
Identify the barriers in the system against collaborative working and the approaches required for effective working together.	○	○	○
Review effective strategies for inclusive, integrated practice.	○	○	○
Reflect on the core skills required for working collaboratively across organisations including during inter-professional meetings.	○	○	○

Chapter 5: Assessment and Risk Management

I can:	Not at all	Partly	Very well
Develop familiarity with contemporary assessment tools for work with children and families.	○	○	○
Utilise developmental theories and models for assessing children and young people's welfare.	○	○	○
Recognise assessment as part of the continuum of care and therapeutic support necessary for safeguarding children and young people.	○	○	○

Understand the key issues and skills relevant to effective risk
management in child protection work.   ○   ○   ○

Chapter 6: The Process of Protection

I can:	Not at all	Partly	Very well
Understand the importance of clear planning and co-ordination for safeguarding children and young people.	○	○	○
Be clear about the stages of the child protection process and the legal framework supporting it.	○	○	○
Develop competence in using the provisions of the Children Act 1989 to safeguard children and young people.	○	○	○
Understand the ways in which the Human Rights Act 1998 can be used to support the welfare of children and young people.	○	○	○

Chapter 7: Supporting Young People's Transition

I can:	Not at all	Partly	Very well
Reflect upon the reason for and effects of risk taking behaviour in young people.	○	○	○
Understand the preparatory work required to support young people through transition from child to adult services.	○	○	○
Reflect on my changing role with the young person during and after transition.	○	○	○
Understand the communication issues and opportunities between practitioners and children and young people.	○	○	○

Chapter 8: Social Inclusion and Cultural Competence

I can:	Not at all	Partly	Very well
Describe what is meant by social inclusion and cultural competence.	○	○	○
Illustrate the importance of anti-discriminatory practice to safeguarding children and young people.	○	○	○
Explain what changes can be made to contemporary practice to meet the needs of a diverse society.	○	○	○
Describe the elements of socially inclusive safeguarding practice.	○	○	○

Chapter 9: Reviewing and Ending Safely

I can:	Not at all	Partly	Very well
Demonstrate the importance and purpose of a child care review.	○	○	○
Understand the significance of enabling the child to express their views.	○	○	○
Ensure that transfer of cases happens speedily with maximum inter-agency communication.	○	○	○
Describe the importance of reflective practice and supervision.	○	○	○

Bibliography

Abrahams, N., Casey, K. and Daro, D. (1992) Teachers' Knowledge, Attitudes and Beliefs About Child Abuse and Its Prevention. *Child Abuse and Neglect.* 16: 2, 229–38.

Adams, A., Erath, P. and Shardlow, S. (2000) *Fundamentals of Social Work in Selected European Countries.* Lyme Regis: Russell House Publishing.

Allan, M., Bhavnani, R. and French, K. (1992) *Promoting Women.* London: Social Services Inspectorate/HMSO.

Audit Commission (1994) *Seen But Not Heard.* London: HMSO.

Audit Commission (2002) *Recruitment Retention: A Public Service Workforce for The Twenty-First Century.* London: Audit Commission.

Bagley, C. and King, K. (1990) *Child Sexual Abuse: The Search for Healing.* London: Tavistock-Routledge.

Baker, K. and Coe, L. (1993) Growing Up With A Chronic Condition: Transition to Young Adulthood for The Individual With Cystic Fibrosis. *Holistic Nurse Practice.* 8: 1, 8–15.

Baldwin, N. (Ed.) (2000) *Protecting Children, Promoting Their Rights.* London: Whiting and Birch.

Bannister, A. and Huntington, A. (2002) *Communicating With Children and Adolescents, Action for Change.* London: Jessica Kingsley.

Baradon, T., Sinason, V. and Yabsley, S. (1999) Assessment of Parents and Young Children: A Child Psychotherapy Point of View. *Child Care Health and Development.* 25: 1, 37–53.

Barford, R. (1993) *Children's View of Child Protection Social Work, Social Work Monographs.* Norwich: University of East Anglia.

Barlow, J. (1998) Parent Training Programmes and Behaviour Problems: Findings From A Systematic Review. In Buchanan, A. and Hudson, B. (Eds.) *Parenting, Schooling, and Childrens Behaviour: Interdisciplinary Approaches.* Alton: Ashgate.

Barnes, M. and Warren, L. (1999) *Paths to Empowerment.* Bristol: Policy Press.

Barry, B. and Hallett, C. (1998) *Social Exclusion and Social Work: Issues and Theory, Policy and Practice.* Lyme Regis: Russell House Publishing.

Barton, A. (2002) *Managing Fragmentation.* Aldershot: Ashgate.

BASW (2003) *BASW Response to The DfES Green Paper: Every Child Matters.* Birmingham: BASW.

Bayley, R. (1999) *Transforming Children's Lives: The Importance of Early Intervention.* London: Family Policy Studies Centre.

Beckett, C. (2003) *Child Protection: An Introduction.* London: Sage.

Bee, H. (1992) *The Developing Child.* 6th edn, New York: Harper Collins.

Bee, H. (1994) *Lifespan Development.* New York: Harper Collins.

Belsky, J. (1980) Child Maltreatment: an Ecological Approach. *American Psychologist.* 35: 320–35.

Bentovim, A. (2002) Working With Abusing Families in Child Abuse: Defining, Understanding and Intervening. In Wilson, K. and James, A. (2002) *The Child Protection Handbook.* London: Balliére Tindall.

Beresford, B., Sloper, P., Baldwin, S. and Newman, T. (1996) *What Works in Services for Families with a Disabled Child.* Ilford: Barnardo's.

Bhugra, D. (1999) *Mental Health of Ethnic Minorities, an Annotated Bibliography.* London: Gaskell.

Bhugra, D. and Bhui, K. (1999) Psychotherapy for Ethnic Minorities. *British Journal of Psychotherapy,* 14: 3, 310–26.

Bhui, K, and Olajide, D. (Eds.) (1999) *Mental Health Service Provision for A Multi-Cultural Society.* London: Saunders.

Bifulco, A. and Moran, P. (1998) *Wednesday's Child, Research Into Women's Experiences of Neglect and Abuse in Childhood, and Adult Depression*. London: Routledge.

Bingley-Miller, L., Fisher, T. and Sinclair, I. (1993) Decisions to Register Children as at Risk of Abuse. *Social Work and Social Science Review*. 4: 2, 101–18.

Birchall, E. and Hallett, C. (1995) *Working Together in Child Protection*. London: HMSO.

Blom-Cooper, L. (1985) *A Child in Trust: The Report of The Panel of Inquiry Into The Circumstances Surrounding The Death of Jasmine Beckford*. London: Borough of Brent.

Blom-Cooper, L. (1987) *A Child in Mind: Protection of Children in A Responsible Society. The Report of The Commission of Inquiry Into The Circumstances Surrounding The Death of Kimberley Carlile*. London: Borough of Greenwich.

Blyth, E. and Cooper, H. (1999) Schools Child Protection. In The Violence Against Children Study Group. *Children, Child Abuse and Child Protection, Placing The Child Centrally*. Chichester: Wiley.

Bochner, S. (1994) Cross-cultural Differences in the Self-concept: A Test of Hofstede's Individualism/Collectivism Distinction. *Journal of Cross-cultural Psychology*, 2, 273–83.

Bourne, D. (1993) Over-Chastisement, Child Non-Compliance and Parenting Skills: A Behavioural Intervention by A Family Centre Social Worker. *British Journal of Social Work*. 5: 481–500.

Brandon, M., Thoburn, J., Lewis, A. and Way, A. (1999) *Safeguarding Children with the Children Act 1989*. London: The Stationery Office.

Braye, S. and Preston-Shoot, M. (1997) *Practising Social Work Law*. 2nd Edition. London: Macmillan.

Browne, K. (2002) Child Abuse: Defining, Understanding and Intervening. In Wilson, K. and James, A. (2002) *The Child Protection Handbook*. London: Balliére Tindall.

Buchanan, A. (2002) Family Support. In McNeish, D., Newman, T. and Roberts, H. (2002) *What Works for Children? Effective Services for Children and Families*. Buckingham: Open University Press.

Buckley, H. (2003) *Child Protection: Beyond The Rhetoric*. London: Jessica Kingsley.

Butler, I. and Roberts, G. (1997) *Social Work With Children and Families: Getting Into Practice*. London: Jessica Kingsley.

Butler-Sloss, E. (1988) *Report of The Inquiry Into Child Abuse in Cleveland, 1987*. London: HMSO.

Calder, M. and Horwath, J. (Eds.) (1999) *Working for Children on The Child Protection Register*. Aldershot: Arena.

Calder, M.C. (2003) The Assessment Framework: A Critique and Reformulation. In Calder, M.C. and Hackett, S. *Assessment in Childcare*. Lyme Regis: Russell House Publishing.

Campbell, B. (1988) *Unofficial Secrets*. London: Virago.

Cannan, C., Berry, L. and Lyons, K. (1992) *Social Work and Europe*. London: Macmillan/BASW.

Carr, A. (2000) *What Works With Children and Adolescents?* London: Routledge.

Casey, A. (1988) A Partnership With Child and Family. *Senior Nurse*. 8: 4, 8–9.

Casey, A. (1993) Development Use of The Partnership Model of Nursing Care. In Glasper, G. and Tucker, A. (1993) *Advances in Child Health Nursing*. London: Scutari Press.

Cawson, P. et al. (2000) *Child Maltreatment in The United Kingdom: A Study of the Prevalence of Child Abuse and Neglect*. London: NSPCC.

Challis, L.S., Fuller, P., Henwood, R., Klein, W., Plowden, A., Webb, P., Whittingham, P. and Wistow, S. *Joint Approaches to Social Policy. Rationality and Practice*. Cambridge: Cambridge University Press.

Chalmers, I. (1994) Assembling The Evidence. In Alderson et al. *What Works? Effective Social Interventions in Child Welfare*. Barkingside: Barnardo's.

Charles, M. and Hendry, E. (2000) *Training Together to Safeguard Children*. London: NSPCC.

Charles, M. with Stevenson, O. (1991) *Multidisciplinary is Different: Sharing Perspectives*. Nottingham: University of Nottingham.

Cheetham, J. et al. (1992) *Evaluating Social Work Effectiveness*. Buckingham: Open University Press.

Chief Inspector of Prisons (2004) *Report on Four Short-term Holding Facilities*. HM Chief Inspector of Prisons.

Children's Society (2002) *Thrown Away.* London: The Children's Society.

Christiansen, E. and James, G. (Eds.) (2000) *Research With Children, Perspectives and Practices.* London: Falmer Press.

Cleaver, H., Unell, I. and Aldgate, J. (1999) *Children's Needs: Parenting Capacity.* London: DoH.

Clifford, D. (1998) *Social Assessment Theory and Practice.* Aldershot: Aldgate Publishing.

Coleman, M., Ganong, L. and Cable, S. (1997) Beliefs About Women's Intergenerational Family Obligations to Provide Support Before and After Divorce and Remarriage. *Journal of Marriage and The Family.* 59: 1, 165–76.

Collins, A. (1998) *Our Children at Risk, Children and Youth Issues.* London: YMCA.

Commission for Health Improvement (2003) *An Audit of Child Protection Arrangements.* London: DoH.

Commission for Social Care Inspection (2004) *Factsheet: Children's Views and Report on Keeping Children Safe From Harm.* London: CSCI.

Conway, S.J. et al. (2000) *Cystic Fibrosis in Children and Adults, The Leeds Method of Management.* Revised edn, Leeds: St James Seacroft University Hospital.

Corby, B. (1987) *Working With Child Abuse.* Milton Keynes: Open University Press.

Corby, B. (2000) *Child Abuse: Towards A Knowledge Base.* 2nd edn, Buckingham: Open University Press.

Corby, B., Millar, M. and Pope, A. (2002) Assessing Children in Need Assessments: A Parental Perspective. *Practice,* 14: 4, 5–16.

Crawford, M. and Kessel, A. (1999) Not Listening to Patients: The Use and Misuse of Patient Satisfaction Studies. *International Journal of Social Psychiatry.* 45: 1, 1–6.

Crisp, S. (1994) *Counting on Families: Social Audit Report on The Provision of Family Support Services.* London: Exploring Parenthood.

Crittenden, P. (1997) Patterns of Attachment and Sexual Behaviour: Risk of Dysfunction Versus Opportunity for Creating Integration. In Atkinson, L. and Zucker, K.J. (Eds.) *Attachment Psychopathology.* New York: Guilford Press.

Dale, P. (2004) Like A Fish in A Bowl: Parents Perceptions of Child Protection Services. *Child Abuse Review.* 13: 137–57.

Dale, P. et al. (1986) *Dangerous Families.* London: Routledge.

Dallos, R, and Draper, R. (2000) *An Introduction to Family Therapy.* Buckingham: Open University Press.

Debell, D. and Everett, G. (1997) *In a Class Apart: A Study of School Nursing.* Norwich: East Norfolk Health Authority.

DeMause, L. (1998) The History of Child Abuse. *The Journal of Psychohistory.* 25: 3 Winter.

Denis, J. and Smith, T. (2002) Nationality, Immigration and the Asylum Bill 2002: Its Impact on Children. *Childright,* 187, 16–7.

Dennehy, A., Smith, L. and Harker, P. (1997) *Not to Be Ignored, Young People, Poverty and Health.* London: Child Poverty Action Group.

Dept for Work and Pensions (2003) *Annual Report.* London: HMSO.

DES (1988) *Child Protection in Schools.* Circular 4/88. London: DES.

DfES (2002) *Don't Suffer in Silence: An Anti-Bullying Pack for Schools.* London: HMSO.

DfES (2003) *Keeping Children Safe.* London: HMSO.

DfES (2003) *The Children Act Report 2002.* Nottingham: DfES Publications.

DfES (2003a) *Children in Need.* London: HMSO.

DfES (2003b) *Every Child Matters.* London: HMSO.

DfES (2004a) *Refocusing Children's Services Towards Prevention: Lessons From The Literature.* London: HMSO.

DfES (2004b) *The Children Act.* Nottingham: DfES Publications.

DfES (2004c) *Every Child Matters: Change for Children.* London: HMSO.

DfES (2005a) *Common Core of Skills and Knowledge for The Children's Workforce.* London: HMSO.

DfES (2005b) *Common Assessment Framework*. London: HMSO.

DHSS (1974) *Non-Accidental Injury to Children*. London: DHSS.

DHSS (1974) *Report of The Committee of Inquiry Into The Care Supervision Provided in Relation to Maria Colwell*. London: HMSO.

DHSS (1983) *Child Abuse: A Study of Inquiry Reports 1973–1981*. London: HMSO.

DHSS (1986) *Child Abuse: Working Together: A Draft Guide to Arrangements for Interagency Cooperation for The Protection of Children*. London: HMSO.

DHSS (1988) *Working Together*. London: HMSO.

Dimigen, G. et al. (1999) Psychiatric Disorder Among Children at Time of Entering Local Authority Care. *British Medical Journal*. 319: 675–6.

Dingwall, R., Eekelaar, J. and Murray, T. (1995) *The Protection of Children: State Intervention and Family Life*. 2nd Edition. London: Avebury.

DoH (1988) *Protecting Children: A Guide for Social Workers Undertaking A Comprehensive Assessment*. London: HMSO.

DoH (1989) *The Children Act 1989*. London: HMSO.

DoH (1989) *The Children Act 1989: an Introductory Guide for The NHS*. London: HMSO.

DoH (1991) *Child Abuse: A Study of Inquiry Reports 1980–1989*. London: HMSO.

DoH (1991) *Family Placements, The Children Act 1989, Guidance Regulations*. London: HMSO.

DoH (1991) *Working Together Under The Children Act 1989*. London: HMSO.

DoH (1995) *Child Protection: Messages From Research*. London: HMSO.

DoH (1997) *General Household Survey*. London: HMSO.

DoH (1998) *Disability Discrimination Act*. London: HMSO.

DoH (1999) *Quality Protects Programme: Transforming Children's Services 2000–01*. London: HMSO.

DoH (1999) *Second Report to The UN Committee on The Rights of The Child by the UK*. London: HMSO.

DoH (1999) *The Protection of Children Act*. London: HMSO.

DoH (1999) *Working Together to Safeguard Children*, London: HMSO.

DoH (2000) *Framework for The Assessment of Children in Need and Their Families*. London: HMSO.

DoH (2000a) *Quality Protects: Disabled Children, Numbers Categories*. London: HMSO.

DoH (2001) *Children (Leaving Care) Act*. London: HMSO.

DoH (2001) *National Plan for Safeguarding Children From Commercial Sexual Exploitation*. London: HMSO.

DoH (2002) *Child in Need Survey*. London: HMSO.

DoH (2003) *Children Looked After by Local Authorities*. London: HMSO.

DoH (2003) *Guidelines for The Appointment of General Practitioners With Special Interests in The Delivery of Clinical Services*. London: DoH Publications.

DoH (2003) *The Victoria Climbié Inquiry*. London: HMSO.

DoH (2003) General Household Survey.

DoH (2003) *What to Do If You Are Worried a Child is Being Abused*. London: DoH Publications.

Dominelli, L. (Ed.) (1999) *Community Approaches to Child Welfare*. Aldershot: Ashgate.

Dominelli, L. (2002) *Anti-oppressive Social Work. Theory and Practice*. Basingstoke: Macmillan.

Durlak, J. (1998) Primary Prevention Programmes for Children and Adolescents Are Effective. *Journal of Mental Health*. 7: 5, 454–69.

Dwivedi, K.W. (2002) *Meeting the Needs of Ethnic Minority Children*. London: Jessica Kingsley.

Eayrs, C. and Jones, R. (1992) Methodological Issues and Future Directions in The Evaluation of Early Intervention Programmes. *Child Care, Health and Development*. 18: 15–28.

Eber, L., Osuch, R. and Redditt, C.A. (1996) School Based Applications of the Wraparound Process: Early Results on Service Provision and Student Outcomes. *Journal of Child and Family Studies*, 5, 83–99.

Eliason, M. (1996) Lesbian and Gay Family Issues. *Journal of Family Nursing*. 2: 1, 10–29.

Elicker, J. et al. (1992) Predicting Peer Competence and Peer Relationships in Childhood From Early Parent-Child Relationships. In Parke, R.D. and Ladd, G.W. (Eds.) *Family-Peer Relationships*. Hillsdale, NJ: Erlbaum.

Evans, M. and Miller, C. (1993) *Partnership in Child Protection*. London: NISW.

Everitt, A. and Hardiker, P. (1996) *Evaluating Good Practice*. Basingstoke: Macmillan.

Farmer, E. and Owen, M. (1995) *Child Protection Practice: Private Risks and Public Remedies*. London: HMSO.

Farrington, D. (1996) *Understanding and Preventing Youth Crime*. York: Joseph Rowntree Foundation.

Favlov, A. (1996) *Study of Working Together "Part 8" Reports, Fatal Child Abuse Parental Psychiatric Disorder*. London: HMSO.

Ferguson, H. and O'Reilly, M. (2001) *Keeping Children Safe, Child Abuse, Child Protection and The Promotion of Welfare*. Dublin: A A Framar.

Fielding, N. and Conroy, S. (1994) Against The Grain: Co-operation in Child Sexual Abuse Investigations. In Stephens, M. and Becker, S. (Eds.) (1994) *Police Force, Police Service: Care and Control in Britain*. Basingstoke: Macmillan.

Fineman, S. (1985) *Social Work Stress and Intervention*. Aldershot: Gower.

Fletcher-Cambell, F. (2001) *Issues of Exclusion: Evidence from Three Recent Research Studies*. Support for Learning, 17: 1, 19–22.

Forrester, D. (2000) Parental Substance Abuse and Child Protection in A British Sample. *Child Abuse Review*, 9: 235–46.

Fox Harding, L. (1991) *Perspectives in Child Care Policy*. London: Longman.

Freeman, I. et al. (1996) Consulting Service Users: The Views of Young People. In Hill, M. and Aldgate, J. (Eds.) *Child Welfare Services: Developments in Law, Policy, Practice and Research*. London: Jessica Kingsley.

Freeman, M. (1984) *State, the Law and The Family*. London: Tavistock.

FRG (1986) FRG's Response to The DHSS Consultation Paper: Child Abuse – Working Together. London: Family Rights Group.

Fulcher, J. and Scott, J. (1999) *Sociology*. Oxford: Oxford University Press.

Fuller, R. (1996) Evaluating Social Work Effectiveness: A Pragmatic Approach. In Alderson et al. *What Works: Effective Social Interventions in Child Welfare*. Barkingside: Barnardo's.

Furniss, T. (1991) *The Multi-Professional Handbook of Child Sexual Abuse*. London: Routledge.

Gadsby Waters, J. (1992) *The Supervision of Child Protection Work*. Aldershot: Avebury.

Gardner, R. (1998) *Family Support: Practitioners Guide*. Birmingham: Venture Press.

Garmezy, N., Masten, A.S. and Tellegren, A. (1984) The Study of Stress and Competence in Children: A Building Block for Developmental Psychotherapy. *Child Development* 5, 97–111.

Garratt, D., Roche, J. and Tucker, S. (Eds.) (1997) *Changing Experiences of Youth*. London: Sage.

George, C. (1996) A Representational Perspective of Child Abuse Prevention: Internal Working Models of Attachment Caregiving. *Child Abuse and Neglect*. 20: 5, 411–24.

Ghated, Daniels, A. (1997) *Talking About My Generation*. London: NSPCC.

Gibbons, J, and Wilding, J. (1995) *Needs, Risks and Family Support Plans: Social Services Departments Responses to Neglected Children*. Norwich: University of East Anglia.

Giller, H., Gormley, C. and Williams, P. (1992) *The Effectiveness of Child Protection Procedures*. Nantwich: Social Information Systems.

Glisson, C. and Hemmelgarn, A. (1998) The Effects of Organisational Climate and Interorganisational Coordination on The Quality and Outcomes of Children's Service Systems. *Child Abuse and Neglect*. 22: 5, 401–21.

GMC (1993) *Confidentiality and Child Abuse*. London: General Medical Council.

Goodman, R. and Scott, S. (1997) *Child Psychiatry*. Oxford: Blackwell Science.

Gordon, G. and Grant, R. (1997) *How We Feel: an Insight Into The Emotional World of Teenagers*. London: Jessica Kingsley.

Gordon, L. (1989) *Heroes of Their Own Lives*. London: Virago.

Gouldner, A. (1954) *Patterns of Industrial Bureaucracy*. New York, NY: Free Press.

Gray, J. (2004) The Interface Between The Child Welfare and Criminal Justice Systems in England. *Child Abuse Review*. 13: 312–23.

Gregg, S. (1995) *Preventing Antisocial Behaviour in At-Risk Students*. OERI.

Griffin, C. (1993) *Representations of Youth: The Study of Youth Adolescence in Britain and America*. Cambridge: Polity Press.

Gross, D., Fogg, L. and Tucker, S. (1995) The Efficacy of Parent Training for Promoting Positive Parent-Toddler Relationships. *Research in Nursing Health*. 18: 489–99.

Guardian, The (2005) *Cautious Doctors Shun Child Protection*. May.

Hallett, C. (1995) *Interagency Coordination in Child Protection*. London: HMSO.

Hallett, C. and Birchall, E. (1992) *Coordination and Child Protection: A Review of The Literature*. London: HMSO.

Hampson, S. (1995) *Individual Differences and Personality*. Longman.

Haralambos, M. and Holborn, (1991) *Sociology: Themes and Perspectives*. 3rd edn, London: Collins.

Harbin, F. and Murphy, M. (Eds.) (2000) *Substance Misuse and Childcare*. Lyme Regis: Russell House Publishing.

Hardiker, P. (1995) *The Social Policy Contexts of Services to Prevent Unstable Family Life*. York: Joseph Rowntree Foundation.

Hardiker, P., Exton, K. and Barker, M. (1991) The Social Policy Contexts of Prevention in Child Care. *British Journal of Social Work*. 21: 341–59.

Harrison, R. et al. (2003) *Partnership Made Painless*. Lyme Regis: Russell House Publishing.

Hellinckx, W., Colton, M. and Williams, M. (1997) *International Perspectives on Family Support*. Aldershot: Ashgate Publishing.

Helman, C, (2001) *Culture, Health and Illness*. London: Arnold.

Hendrick, H. (Ed.) (2005) *Child Welfare and Social Policy, an Essential Reader*. Bristol: Policy Press.

Hennessey, E. (1999) Children as Service Evaluators. *Child Psychology and Psychiatry Review*. 4: 153–61.

Hern, M.M. et al. (1998) Sensitive Topics and Adolescents: Making Research About Risk Taking Behaviours Happen. *Issues in Comprehensive Pediatric Nursing*. 21: 173–86.

Hill, M. (1999) *Effective Ways of Working With Children and Their Families*. London: Jessica Kingsley.

Hill, M., Laybourn, A. and Borl, M. (1996) Engaging With Primary-Age Children About Their Emotions and Well-Being: Methodological Considerations. *Children Society*. 10: 129–44.

Holler, H. (2002) Psychodramas With 'At Risk' Youth: A Means of Active Engagement. In Bannister, A. and Huntington, A. *Communicating With Children and Adolescents, Action for Change*. London: Jessica Kingsley.

Holt, C. (1998) Working With Fathers of Children in Need. In Bayley R. (Ed.) *Transforming Children's Lives: The Importance of Early Intervention*. London. Family Policy Studies Centre.

Holterman, S. (1995) *All Our Futures: The Impact of Public Expenditure and Fiscal Policies on Britain's Children and Young People*. Barkingside: Barnardo's.

Home Office (1988) *The Investigation of Child Sexual Abuse*. London:Home Office.

Home Office (1996) *National Commission of Enquiry into the Prevention of Child Abuse: Childhood Matters*. London: HMSO.

Home Office (1997) *Social Trends*. London: HMSO.

Home Office (2004) *The Bichard Report*. London: HMSO.

Home Office/DoH (2001) *Achieving Best Evidence in Criminal Proceedings*. London: HMSO.

House of Commons (1997) *Child and Adolescent Mental Health Services*. London: HMSO.

House of Lords (1986) *Gillick V West Norfolk Wisbech Area Health Authority*. 1 AC 112.

Howarth, J. (2002) *The Childs World: Assessment of Children in Need*. London: Jessica Kingsley.

Howe, D. (1986) Social Workers and Their Practice. In *Welfare Bureaucracies*. Aldershot: Gower.

Howe, D. (1989) *The Consumers View of Family Therapy*. London: Gower.

Howe, D. et al. (1999) *Attachment Theory, Child Maltreatment and Family Support*. Basingstoke: Macmillan.

Hugman, R. (1991) *Power in the Caring Professions*. London: Macmillan.

Iwaniec, D. (1995) *The Emotionally Abused and Neglected Child: Identification, Assessment and Intervention*. Chichester: Wiley.

Jack, G. (2004) Child Protection at The Community Level. *Child Abuse Review*. 13: 368–83.

Jack, R. and Walker, S. (2000) *Social Work Assessment and Intervention*. Cambridge: APU.

JCWI (2002) *Immigration, Nationality and Refugee Law Handbook*. London: Joint Council for the Welfare of Immigrants.

Jones, D. and Jones, M. (1999) The Assessment of Children with Emotional and Behavioural Difficulties: Psychometrics and Beyond. In Cooper, P. (Ed.) *Understanding and Supporting Children with Emotional and Behavioural Difficulties*. London: Jessica Kingsley.

Jones, D.P.H. (1997) Treatment of the Child and the Family where Child Abuse and Neglect has Occurred. In Helfer, R., Kempe, R. and Krugman, R. (Eds.) *The Battered Child*. 5th Edition. Chicago: University of Chicago Press.

Jones, L. and O'Loughlin, T. (2002) Developing A Child Concern Model to Embrace The Framework. In Calder, M.C. and Hackett, S. (Eds.) *The Child Care Assessment Manual*. Lyme Regis: Russell House Publishing.

Kay, J. (1999) *A Practical Guide: Protecting Children*. London: Cassell.

Kay, J. (2003) *Protecting Children: A Practical Guide*. London: Continuum.

Kearney, P., Levin, E. and Rosen, G. (2000) *Alcohol, Drug and Mental Health Problems: Working with Families*. London: National Institute for Social Work.

Kelson, M. (1995) *Consumer Involvement Initiatives in Clinical Audit Outcomes*. London: College of Health.

Kempe, C.H. et al. (1962) The Battered Child Syndrome. *Journal of The American Medical Association*. 181: 17–22.

Kemps, C. (1997) Approaches to Working With Ethnicity and Cultural Issues. In Dwivedi, K. (Ed.) *Enhancing Parenting Skills*. London: Wiley.

Kiddle, C. (1999) *Traveller Children: A Voice for Themselves*. London: Jessica Kingsley.

Kim, W.J. (1995) A Training Guideline of Cultural Competence for Child and Adolescent Psychiatric Residences. *Child Psychiatry and Human Development* 21.

Kotch, J.B. et al. (1993) Morbidity and Death Due to Child Abuse in New Zealand. *Child Abuse and Neglect*. 17: 2, 233–47.

Kurtz, Z. (1996) *Treating Children Well: A Guide to Using The Evidence Base in Commissioning and Managing Services for The Mental Health of Children and Young People*. London: Mental Health Foundation.

Kyngas, H., Hentinen, M. and Barlow, J.H. (1998) Adolescents Perception of Physicians, Nurses, Parents and Friends. *Journal of Advanced Nursing*. 27: 760–9.

Laming, H. (2003) *The Inquiry Into The Death of Victoria Climbié*. London: HMSO.

Lansdowne, G. (1995) *Taking Part: Children's Participation in Decision-Making*. London: IPPR.

Laufer, M. (1985) (Ed.) *The Suicidal Adolescent*. London: Karnac Books.

Leathard, A. (Ed.) (1994) *Going Inter-professional. Working together for Health and Welfare*. London: Routledge.

Leonard, P. (1997) *Post-modern Welfare: Reconstructing an Emancipatory Project*. London: Sage.

Leutz, W.N. (1999) Five Laws for Integrating Medical and Social Services: Lessons from the United States and the United Kingdom. *Millbank Quarterly* 77: 77–110.

Lindon, J. (2003) *Child Protection*. 2nd edn, London: Hodder Stoughton.

Little, M. and Mount, K. (1999) *Prevention and Early Intervention With Children in Need*. Aldershot: Ashgate.

Lloyd, E. (1999) (Ed.) *Parenting Matters: What Works in Parenting Education?* London: Barnardo's.

Lyon, C. and De Cruz, R. (1993) *Child Abuse.* 2nd edn, Bristol: Jordan.

Lyon, J., Dennison, C. and Wilson, A. (2000) *Tell Them so They Listen: Messages from Young People in Custody.* Home Office Research Study 21. London: HMSO.

MacDonald, G. (2002) Child Protection. In McNeish, D., Newman, T. and Roberts, H. (2002) *What Works for Children? Effective Services for Children and Families.* Open University Press: Buckingham.

MacDonald, G. and Roberts, H. (1995) *What Works in The Early Years? Effective Interventions for Children and Their Families.* Barkingside: Barnardo's.

Madge, N. (2001) *Understanding Difference – The Meaning of Ethnicity for Young Lives.* London: National Children's Bureau.

Magrab, P., Evans, P. and Hurrell, P. (1997) Integrated Services for Children and Youth at Risk: An International Study of Multi-disciplinary Training. *Journal of Inter-professional Care,* 11: 1, 99–108.

Marsh, P. and Crow, G. (1998) *Family Group Conferences in Child Welfare.* Oxford: Blackwell Science.

Mayseless, O. (1996) Attachment Patterns Their Outcomes. *Human Development.* 36: 206–23.

McGlone, F., Park, A. and Smith, K. (1998) *Families and Kinship.* London: Family Policy Studies Centre.

McNeish, D. and Newman, T. (2002) Involving Children and Young People in Decision Making. In McNeish, D, Newman, T. and Roberts, H. (Eds.) *What Works for Children?* Buckingham: Open University Press.

Mental Health Foundation (1999) *The Big Picture: Promoting Children and Young People's Mental Health.* London: Mental Health Foundation.

Mental Health Foundation (2002) *The Mental Health Needs of Young Offenders.* London: MHF.

Micklewright, J. and Stewart, K. (2000) *Well-Being of Children in The European Union New Economy.* London: Institute for Public Policy Research.

Middleton, L. (1997) *The Art of Assessment.* Birmingham: Venture Press.

Miller, G. and Prinz, R. (1990) Enhancement of Social Learning Family Interventions for Childhood Conduct Disorders. *Psychological Bulletin.* 108. 291–307.

Milner, J. and O'Byrne, P. (1998) *Assessment in Social Work Practice.* London: Macmillan.

Modood, T. and Berthoud, R. (1997) *Ethnic Minorities in Britain.* London: Policy Studies Institute.

Moffic, H.S. and Kinzie, J.D. (1996) The History and Future of Cross-cultural Psychiatric Services. *Community Mental Health Journal,* 32, 581–92.

Moore, J. (1992) *The ABC of Child Protection.* Aldershot: Ashgate.

Morris, J. (1998) *Accessing Human Rights: Disabled Children and the Children Act.* Ilford: Barnardo's.

Morris, J. (2000) *Having Someone Who Cares? Barriers to Change in The Public Care of Children.* London: NCB.

Morrison, T. (1993) *Supervision in Social Care.* London: Longman.

Morrison, T. (1997) Emotionally Competent Child Protection Organisations: Fallacy, Fiction or Necessity. In Bates, J., Pugh, R. and Thompson, N. *Protecting Children: Challenges and Change.* Aldershot: Arena.

Morrow, V. (1998) *Understanding Families: Children's Perspectives.* London: NCB.

Moules, T. and Ramsay, J. (1998) *The Textbook of Children's Nursing.* Cheltenham: Stanley Thornes Ltd.

Mrazek, P.J., Lynch, M.A. and Bentovim, A. (1983) Sexual Abuse of Children in the United Kingdom. *Child Abuse and Neglect* 7, 147–53.

Munro, E. (2002) *Effective Child Protection.* London: Sage Publications.

Murphy, M. (1996) *The Child Protection Unit.* Aldershot: Avebury.

Murphy, M. (1997) Staff Care in A Multidisciplinary Context. In Bates, J. et al., *Protecting Children: Challenges and Change.* Aldershot: Arena.

Murphy, M. (2000) The Interagency Trainer. In Charles, M. and Hendry, E. *Training Together to Safeguard Children.* London: NSPCC.

Murphy, M. (2003) Keeping Going. In Harrison, R. et al., *Partnership Made Painless.* Lyme Regis: Russell House Publishing.

Murphy, M. (2004) *Developing Collaborative Relationships in Inter-agency Child Protection Work*. 2nd Edition. Lyme Regis: Russell House Publishing.

Murphy, M. and Oulds, G. (2000) Establishing and Developing Co-operative Links Between Substance Misuse and Child Protection Systems. In Harbin, F. and Murphy, M. (Eds.) *Substance Misuse in Childcare*. Lyme Regis: Russell House Publishing.

Murray, A. (1997) The Effects of Infant's Behaviour on Maternal Mental Health. *Health Visitor*. 66: 2, Feb.

National Commission of Inquiry Into the Prevention of Child Abuse (1996) London: HMSO.

NCB (2005) *Social Inclusion*. London: NCB.

NCH (1979) *Who Cares?* London: NCH.

NCH (2000) *Fact File*. London: NCH.

Norman, A. and Brown, C. (1992) Foreword. In Cloke, C. and Naish, J. (Eds.) *Key Issues in Child Protection for Health Visitors Nurses*. London: NSPCC/Longman.

NSPCC (1996) *Childhood Matters: The Report of The National Commission of Inquiry Into The Prevention of Child Abuse*. London: HMSO.

NSPCC (2000) *Child Maltreatment in The United Kingdom*. London: NSPCC.

Oberhuemer, P. (1998) *Controversies, Chances and Challenges: Reflections on the Quality Debate in Germany*. London: Routledge.

O'Hagan, K. (1989) *Working With Child Sexual Abuse*. Milton Keynes: Open University Press.

O'Hagan, K. (1993) *Emotional and Psychological Abuse of Children*. Buckingham: Open University Press.

Office of Population, Censuses Surveys (1992) *The British Census 1991*. London: HMSO.

Papatheophilou, A. (1990) Child Protection in Greece. In Sale, A. and Davies, M. (Eds.) *Child Protection Policies and Practice in Europe*. London: NSPCC.

Parkinson, J. (1992) Supervision Vs Control. In Cloke, C. and Naish, J. (Eds.) *Key Issues in Child Protection for Health Visitors Nurses*. London: NSPCC/Longman.

Parton, N. (1985) *The Politics of Child Abuse*. Basingstoke: Macmillan.

Parton, N. (1991) *Governing The Family*. Basingstoke: Macmillan.

Parton, N. (1999) Reconfiguring Child Welfare Practices: Risk, Advanced Liberalism and The Government of Freedom. In Chambon, A., Irving, A. and Epstein, L. (Eds.) *Reading Foucault for Social Work*. Chichester: Columbia Press.

Parton, N. (2002) *Discovery and Inclusion*. Submission to The Victoria Climbié Inquiry Phase 2 Seminar 1.

Peace, G. (1991) *Inter-Professional Collaboration, Professional Personal Perspectives, Part 2*. Manchester: Boys' Girls' Welfare Society.

Pearce, J. (2000) Front-Line Workers Faced Pressures of Isolation, Lack of Support and Chaos. *Community Care*. Feb.

Peters, R. and Barlow, J. (2003) Systematic Review of Screening Instruments to Identify Child Abuse during the Perinatal Period. *Child Abuse Review*, 12.

Pickett, J. (Individual Interview, 2 April 1990) in Murphy, M. (1996) *Child Protection Specialist Units*. Aldershot: Avebury.

Pickett, J. and Maton, A. (1979) The Interagency Team in an Urban Setting: The Special Unit Concept. *Child Abuse and Neglect*, 3, 115–21.

Pierson, J. (2002) *Tackling Social Exclusion*. London: Routledge.

Pitts, J. (2001) Korrectional Karaoke: New Labour and The Zombification of Youth Justice. *Youth Justice*. 1: 2.

Plotnikoff, J. (1993) *The Child Witness Pack: Helping Children to Cope*. London: NSPCC/Childline.

Plummer, D.C. (2001) The Quest for Modern Manhood: Masculine Stereotypes, Peer Culture and The Social Significance of Homophobia. *Journal of Adolescence*. 24: 15–23.

Polnay, J. and Blair, M. (1999) A Model Programme for Busy Learners. *Child Abuse Review*. 8: 284–8.

Powell, J. and Lovelock, R. (1992) *Changing Patterns of Mental Health Care*. London: Avebury.

Procter, S. et al. (1998) *Preparation for The Development and Role of The Community Children's Nurse.* London: English National Board.

Pugh, G, and Smith, C. (1996) *Learning to Be A Parent.* London: Family Policy Studies Centre.

Ramon, S. (1999) Social Work. In Bhui, K. and Olajide, D. (Eds.) *Mental Health Service Provision for a Multi-cultural Society.* London: Saunders.

RCP (1991) *Physical Signs of Sexual Abuse in Children.* London: Royal College of Physicians.

Reder, P. and Duncan, S. (2003) Understanding Communication in Child Protection Networks. *Child Abuse Review.* 12: 82–100.

Reder, P. and Lucey, (1995) *Assessment of Parenting, Psychiatric and Psychological Contributions.* London: Routledge.

Reder, P., Duncan, S, and Gray, M. (1993) *Beyond Blame: Child Abuse Tragedies Revisited.* London: Routledge.

Revans, L. (2002a) Laming Probe Reveals Scope of Communications Breakdown. *Community Care.* Feb.

Revans, L. (2002b) Social Services Take on Wider Role as Councils Combine Departments. *Community Care.* Aug.

Richards, M., Payne, C. and Shepperd, A. (1990) *Staff Supervision in Child Protection Work.* London: NISW.

Riley, R. (1997) Working Together: Inter-Professional Collaboration. *Journal of Child Health.* Winter.

Robbins, D. (1998) The Refocusing Children's Services Initiative: an Overview of Practice. In Bayley, R. (Ed.) *Transforming Children's Lives: The Importance of Early Intervention.* London: Family Policy Studies Centre.

Rogers, C. (2003) *Children at Risk 2002–2003: Government Initiatives and Commentaries on Government Policy.* National Family Parenting Institute.

Roth, A. and Fonagy, P. (1996) *What Works for Whom? A Critical Review of Psychotherapy Research.* London: Guilford Press.

Royal College of Psychiatrists (2002) *Parent-Training Programmes for the Management of Young Children with Conduct Disorders, Findings from Research.* RCP.

Ruddock, M. (1998) Yes But, Then Again Maybe. In Davies, R. (Ed.) *Stress in Social Work.* London: Jessica Kingsley.

Rutter, M, and Smith, D. (1995) *Psychosocial Disorders in Young People: Time Trends and Their Causes.* London: Wiley.

Rutter, M. (1985) Resiliance in The Face of Adversity. *British Journal of Psychiatry.* 147: 598–611.

Rutter, M. (1995) *Psychosocial Disturbances in Young People: Challenges for Prevention.* Cambridge: Cambridge University Press.

Rutter, M., Hersov, L. and Taylor, E. (1994) *Child and Adolescent Psychiatry.* Oxford: Blackwell Scientific.

Ryan, M. (1999) *The Children Act 1989: Putting it into Practice.* 2nd Aldershot: Ashgate.

Sale, A. and Davies, M. (Eds.) (1990) *Child Protection Policies and Practice in Europe.* London: NSPCC.

Salford Centre for Social Work Research (2004) *Education and Training for Inter-Agency Working: New Standards.* Manchester: University of Salford.

Salmon, D. and Hall, C. (1999) Working With Lesbian Mothers: Their Healthcare Experiences. *Community Practitioner.* 72: 12, 396–7.

Sariola, H. and Uutela, A. (1993) The Prevalence and Context of Family Violence Against Children in Finland. *Child Abuse and Neglect.* 16: 6, 823–32.

Sbaek, M. (1999) Children With Problems: Focusing on Everyday Life. *Children and Society.* 13, 106–18.

SCARE (2004) *Preventing Teenage Pregnancy in Looked After Children.* SCARE.

Scott, D. (1997) Interagency Conflict: an Ethnographic Study. *Child and Family Social Work.* 2: 2, 73–80.

Scrine, J. (1991) 'Child Abuse – Do Social Work Students Get Enough Practice Experience?', *Practice,* 5(2): 153–9.

Shah, R. (1992) *The Silent Majority: Children with Disabilities in Asian Families.* London: National Children's Bureau.

Walker, S. (2001) Developing Child and Adolescent Mental Health Services. *Journal of Child Health Care.* 5: 2. 71–6.

Walker, S. (2001) Domestic Violence: Analysis of A Community Safety Alarm System. *Child Abuse Review.* 10: 3, 170–82.

Walker, S. (2001c) Tracing the Contours of Postmodern Social Work. *British Journal of Social Work.* 31, 29–39.

Walker, S. (2002) Family Support and Social Work Practice: Renaissance or Retrenchment? *European Journal of Social Work.* 5: 1, 43–54.

Walker, S. (2003) Interprofessional Work in Child and Adolescent Mental Health Services. *Emotional and Behavioural Difficulties.* 8: 3, 189–204.

Walker, S. (2003) *Working Together for Healthy Young Minds.* Lyme Regis: Russell House Publishing.

Walker, S. (2005) *Culturally Competent Therapy: Working With Children and Young People.* Basingstoke: Palgrave Macmillan.

Walker, S. and Akister, J. (2004) *Applying Family Therapy: A Guide for Caring Professionals in The Community.* Lyme Regis: Russell House Publishing.

Walker, S. and Beckett, C. (2004) *Social Work Assessment and Intervention.* Lyme Regis: Russell House Publishing.

Walters, S. and Warren, R. (2001) *Cystic Fibrosis in Adults: A Millennium Survey.* Bromley: Cystic Fibrosis Trust.

Warner, N. (1993) *Choosing With Care.* London: HMSO.

Wattam, C. (1999) The Prevention of Child Abuse. *Children and Society.* 13: 317–29.

Webb, S.A. (2001) Some Considerations on The Validity of Evidence-Based Practice in Social Work. *British Journal of Social Work.* 31, 57–79.

Webster-Stratton, C. (1997) Treating Children With Early-Onset Conduct Problems: A Comparison of Child Parent Training Interventions. *Journal of Consulting Clinical Psychology.* 65: 1, 93–109.

Werner, E. (2000) Protective Factors and Individual Resilience. In *Handbook of Early Childhood Interventions.* 2nd edn, Cambridge: Cambridge University Press.

White, K. and Grove, M. (2000) Towards an Understanding of Partnership. *NCVCCO Outlook.* Issue 7.

Wilson, K. and James, A. (2002) *The Child Protection Handbook.* London: Balliére Tindall.

Woodhead, M., Faulkner, D. and Littleton, D. (Eds.) (1998) *Cultural Worlds of Early Childhood.* London: Routledge.

Wright, S. (2004) Child Protection in The Community: A Community Development Approach. *Child Abuse Review.* 13: 384–98.

Useful Resources and Organisations

Advisory Centre for Education
1b Aberdeen Studios,
22 Highbury Grove, London, N5 2EA
Tel: 020 7354 8321

Asian Family Counselling Services
74 The Avenue, London, W13 8LB
Tel: 020 8997 5749

Asylum Aid
244a Upper Street, London N1 1RU
Tel: 020 7359 4026
www.asylumaid.org.uk

Barnardos
Tanners Lane, Barkingside, IG6 1QG
Tel: 020 8550 8822
www.barnardos.ie

Black Information Link
The 1990 Trust, 9 Cranmer Road,
London SW9 6EJ
Tel: 020 7582 1990
www.blink.org.uk

Child Poverty Action Group
1–5 Bath Street, London EC1V 9PY
Tel: 020 7253 3406

Child Psychotherapy Trust
104 Grafton Road, London NW5 4BD
Tel: 020 7284 1355
www.cpt.co.uk

Childline
2nd Floor, Royal Mail Building,
50 Studd Street, London N1 0QW
Tel: 020 7239 1000
www.childline.org.uk

Children's Legal Centre
University of Essex, Wivenhoe Park
Colchester CO4 3SQ
Tel: 01206 873820
www.essex.ac.uk/clc

Children's Rights Office
City Road, London EC1V 1LJ
Tel: 020 7278 8222
www.cro.org.uk

Children's Society
Edward Rudolf House, Margery Street
London WC1X 0JL
Tel: 020 7841 4436
www.the-childrens-society.org.uk

Commission for Racial Equality
10 Allington Street, London SW1E 5EH
Tel: 020 7828 7022
www.cre.gov.uk

Coram Family
49 Mecklenburgh Square,
London WC1N 2QA
Tel: 020 7520 0300
www.coram.org.uk

Disability Now
6 Market Road, London N7 9PW
0207619 7323
www.disabilitynow.org.uk

Drugscope
32 Longman Street, London SE1 0EE
Tel: 020 7928 1771
www.drugscope.org.uk

FOCUS
The Royal College of Psychiatrists,
6th Floor, 83 Victoria Street,
London SW1H 0HW
Tel: 020 7227 0821
www.rcpsych.ac.uk/cru

Families Need Fathers
134 Curtain Road, London EC2A 3AR
020 7613 5060
www.fnf.org.uk

Family Rights Group
18 Ashwin Street, London E8 3DL
Tel: 020 7923 2628
www.frg.co.uk

Home Start
2 Salisbury Road, Leicester LE1 7QR
Tel: 011 6233 9955
www.home-start.org.uk

Institute of Family Therapy
24 Stephenson Way, London NW1 2HV
Tel: 020 7391 9150
www.ift.org.uk

Kidscape
2 Grosvenor Gdns., London SW1W 9TR
Tel: 020 7730 3300
www.kidscape.org.uk

MIND
15 Broadway, Stratford, London E15 4BQ
Tel: 020 8522 1728
www.mind.org.uk

Mental Health Foundation
20 Cornwall Terrace, London NW1 4QL
Tel: 020 7535 7400
www.mentalhealth.org.uk

NCH Action for Children
85 Highbury Park, London N5 1UD
Tel: 020 7704 7000
www.nchafc.org.uk

NSPCC
42 Curtain Road, London EC2A 3NH
Tel: 020 7825 2500
www.nspcc.org.uk

NAFSIYAT
278 Seven Sisters Road,
London, N4 2HY
020 7263 4130

**National Association of Young People's
Counselling and Advisory Services**
17–23 Albion Road, Leicester, LE1 6GD
Tel: 01642 816846

National Autistic Society
393 City Road
London EC1V 1NE
Tel: 020 7833 2299

National Centre for Eating Disorders
54 New Road, Esher, KT10 9NU
Tel: 01372 469493
www.eating-disorders.org.uk

National Children's Bureau
8 Wakley Street, London EC1V 7QE
Tel: 020 7843 6000
www.ncb.org.uk

National Family and Parenting Institute
520 Highgate Studios, 53–79 Highgate Road,
Kentish Town, London NW5 1TL
Tel: 020 7424 3460
www.nfpi.org.uk

National Pyramid Trust
204 Church Road, London W7 3BP
Tel: 020 8579 5108

Parentline Plus
Unit 520, 53–79 Highgate Road
London NW5 1TL
Tel: 020 7209 2460
www.parentlineplus.org.uk

Race Equality Unit
Unit 27/28, Angel Gate, City Road,
London EC1V 2PT
Tel: 020 7278 2331
www.reunet.demon.co.uk

Refugee Council
3–9 Bondway, London SW8 1SJ
Tel: 020 7820 3000

Save the Children
17 Grove Lane, London SE5 8RD
Tel: 020 7703 5400
www.savethechildren.org.uk

Stepfamilies UK
www.stepfamilies.co.uk

Tavistock Institute
120 Belsize Lane, London NW3 5BA
0207 435 7111
www.tav-port.org.uk

Trust for the Study of Adolescence
23 New Road, Brighton, BN1 1WZ
Tel: 01273 693311
www.tsa.uk.com

Values into Action
Derbyshire Street, London, E2 6HG
Tel: 020 7729 5436

Voice for the Child in Care
4 Pride Court, 80–82 White Lion Street
London N1 9PF
Tel: 020 7833 5792

Who Cares Trust
152 City Road, London EC1V 2NP
Tel: 020 7251 3117
www.thewhocarestrust.org.uk

Women's Aid Federation
PO Box 391, Bristol BS99 7WS
08457 023468
YMCA Dads and Lads Project
25 Lower Bridge St, Chester CH1 1RS
Tel: 01244 403090

Young Minds
102 Clerkenwell Road,
London EC1M 5SA
Tel: 020 7336 8445
www.youngminds.org.uk

Youth Access
2 Taylors Yard, 67 Alderbrook Road,
London SW12 8AD
Tel: 020 8772 9900
www.yacess.co.uk

Youth in Mind
www.youthinmind.net

Photocopiable Activities

Organisations may reproduce the material from this section for training but only for their own local internal use. The source, author and publishers must be credited. Trainers wishing to use this material may do so but should always provide the organisation to whom they are providing any training materials that are copied from this manual, with a copy of the entire manual. Reproduction for any other purpose requires the prior permission of the copyright holder and the publisher.

Activity 1.1

Make space and time at your next team meeting or staff conference to include a discussion on the changes taking place within children's services. Try drawing up two lists: advantages and disadvantages and then build in future time to tackle the perceived disadvantages.

Reproduced from Walker, S. and Thurston, C. *Safeguarding Children and Young People* (RHP, 2006)
ISBN: 1-903855-90-4. www.russellhouse.co.uk

Activity 1.2

Obtain a copy of your agency safeguarding children procedures and practice guidelines, or make sure you know where it is held and to whom you should refer in cases involving child protection.

Reproduced from Walker, S. and Thurston, C. *Safeguarding Children and Young People* (RHP, 2006)
ISBN: 1-903855-90-4. www.russellhouse.co.uk

Activity 1.3

Consider ways in which your agency currently consults with children and young people about the service you provide. They may range from simple feedback forms available upon request or a more pro-active process of inviting comments from representative groups that are officially recorded in statistically meaningful ways. Together with a colleague think of ways consultation could be improved.

Reproduced from Walker, S. and Thurston, C. *Safeguarding Children and Young People* (RHP, 2006) ISBN: 1-903855-90-4. www.russellhouse.co.uk

Activity 1.4

Make an effort to link up with a practitioner from another agency and meet to discuss the seven operational standards and draw up an action plan to present to each other's teams to tackle the barriers to better collaboration.

Reproduced from Walker, S. and Thurston, C. *Safeguarding Children and Young People* (RHP, 2006) ISBN: 1-903855-90-4. www.russellhouse.co.uk

Activity 2.1

Reflect upon the families that you work with; spend time highlighting the different styles of family structure. Analyse each structure exploring the strengths and weaknesses.

Are there any common themes for the families?

Reproduced from Walker, S. and Thurston, C. *Safeguarding Children and Young People* (RHP, 2006)
ISBN: 1-903855-90-4. www.russellhouse.co.uk

Activity 2.2

Compile a list of the useful primary preventive resources you have in the community you work in. Highlight the most popular resources used.

Compare these services and find the similarities that make the services popular.

Reproduced from Walker, S. and Thurston, C. *Safeguarding Children and Young People* (RHP, 2006)
ISBN: 1-903855-90-4. www.russellhouse.co.uk

Activity 2.3

Find a copy of your job description and reflect upon which parts of your practice is undertaken at primary, secondary, tertiary and quaternary level. Where you are working at higher levels, consider ways you may be able to start preventive work earlier.

If you are working at the primary preventive level, how can you utilise services and child care practitioners at the higher levels, to reduce the risk of progression for the children and families you work with?

Reproduced from Walker, S. and Thurston, C. *Safeguarding Children and Young People* (RHP, 2006) ISBN: 1-903855-90-4. www.russellhouse.co.uk

Activity 2.4

Drawing from the list of early intervention skills on page 31 highlight which skills you use most often.

Reflect upon areas that you need to work on to improve.

Develop some strategies to ensure that you are able to use your skills to the best of your ability.

Reproduced from Walker, S. and Thurston, C. *Safeguarding Children and Young People* (RHP, 2006) ISBN: 1-903855-90-4. www.russellhouse.co.uk

Activity 3.1

Spend 5 to 10 minutes reflecting on the community and families you work with, highlight both the general and the geographical specific factors which may lead to children, and young people within your area being at risk.

Could this list contain different risk factors if a colleague from a different agency or organisation undertook this activity?

Reproduced from Walker, S. and Thurston, C. *Safeguarding Children and Young People* (RHP, 2006) ISBN: 1-903855-90-4. www.russellhouse.co.uk

Activity 3.2

Think of a child you have supported who appears to have coped well with the abuse they have survived. List the resilience factors they may have. Compare this with a child who was not able to cope so well.

Reflect upon how the knowledge that you now have may enable you to give appropriate early intervention in the future.

Reproduced from Walker, S. and Thurston, C. *Safeguarding Children and Young People* (RHP, 2006) ISBN: 1-903855-90-4. www.russellhouse.co.uk

Activity 3.3

Using the meanings of the behaviours listed on page 40 and 41 give examples of how you think this is acted out in the family.

When exploring the behaviour of the abuser who is emotionally abusing a child or young person, spend time reflecting on how this may make the child feel.

Reproduced from Walker, S. and Thurston, C. *Safeguarding Children and Young People* (RHP, 2006)
ISBN: 1-903855-90-4. www.russellhouse.co.uk

Activity 3.4

Abigail age 9 years old discloses to you that her daddy comes in to her bed at night and touches her. How would you ensure that she is given the opportunity to tell her story in a safe way, and how would you proceed following the event?

Reproduced from Walker, S. and Thurston, C. *Safeguarding Children and Young People* (RHP, 2006)
ISBN: 1-903855-90-4. www.russellhouse.co.uk

Activity 3.5

Melena is 4 months old and was born one month premature. Mum, who speaks very little English, has brought her to the health centre, as she is concerned that she is not really gaining any weight. She looks pale and withdrawn, and appears thin, and she is dressed in inadequate clothing. Mum says she is always hungry, and is consistently afflicted with minor illness.

How can support for mum be offered that ensures the child's and the entire family's needs are taken into account, including health promotion advice, interpretation, health and social assessment.

Reproduced from Walker, S. and Thurston, C. *Safeguarding Children and Young People* (RHP, 2006) ISBN: 1-903855-90-4. www.russellhouse.co.uk

Activity 4.1

Make a list of all the individuals you work with, remember, to note not just the practitioners you work with on a daily or weekly basis, but those professionals who you may contact infrequently.

Within your practice area reflect upon the barriers that you can see in working effectively with all your colleagues both within your agency and across agencies.

Reproduced from Walker, S. and Thurston, C. *Safeguarding Children and Young People* (RHP, 2006) ISBN: 1-903855-90-4. www.russellhouse.co.uk

Activity 4.2

Reflect upon the team you work in; highlight all the commonalities you share, including qualifications, knowledge and experience. Now highlight all the differences you may have.

Compare and contrast how these similarities and differences bring strengths and weakness to the group.

Reproduced from Walker, S. and Thurston, C. *Safeguarding Children and Young People* (RHP, 2006) ISBN: 1-903855-90-4. www.russellhouse.co.uk

Activity 4.3

Reflect upon the last case conference or inter-professional meeting you attended, drawing on the points highlighted on page 56 for individual stategies for improving communication. Give an honest critique of your performance. What did you do well and what were you unhappy about?

Write yourself some notes and points specifically for how you may change your practice at these meetings in the future.

Reproduced from Walker, S. and Thurston, C. *Safeguarding Children and Young People* (RHP, 2006) ISBN: 1-903855-90-4. www.russellhouse.co.uk

Activity 4.4

List the resources in your area which enable you to get together with colleagues across organisations; this should include formal meetings and informal opportunities.

Keep a diary and make a commitment to contact a variety of colleagues in other organisations on a regular basis.

Reproduced from Walker, S. and Thurston, C. *Safeguarding Children and Young People* (RHP, 2006) ISBN: 1-903855-90-4. www.russellhouse.co.uk

Activity 5.1

Review the above material and make a note of those elements that are less familiar to you. Make sure you make time soon to discuss these in supervision or with your manager to help you understand them and integrate them into your practice.

Reproduced from Walker, S. and Thurston, C. *Safeguarding Children and Young People* (RHP, 2006) ISBN: 1-903855-90-4. www.russellhouse.co.uk

Activity 5.2

Together with a colleague discuss your experiences of the Framework for Assessment of Children in Need for 20 minutes. Come up with three improvements you would like to make and present them to your next team meeting.

Reproduced from Walker, S. and Thurston, C. *Safeguarding Children and Young People* (RHP, 2006) ISBN: 1-903855-90-4. www.russellhouse.co.uk

Activity 5.3

Write down the ways in which you think the guidance will help in your assessment of a child and family you might be working with, and the ways in which this guidance will hinder the assessment.

Reproduced from Walker, S. and Thurston, C. *Safeguarding Children and Young People* (RHP, 2006) ISBN: 1-903855-90-4. www.russellhouse.co.uk

Activity 5.4

Make some brief notes describing several disadvantages of viewing risk solely as danger and intervention as about risk control.

Reproduced from Walker, S. and Thurston, C. *Safeguarding Children and Young People* (RHP, 2006) ISBN: 1-903855-90-4. www.russellhouse.co.uk

Activity 6.1

Discuss a recent assessment with a colleague or supervisor and reflect back on how you did it. Identify three areas for improvement and the means for doing so.

Reproduced from Walker, S. and Thurston, C. *Safeguarding Children and Young People* (RHP, 2006) ISBN: 1-903855-90-4. www.russellhouse.co.uk

Activity 6.2

Together with a colleague consider the case illustration on pages 85 and 86 and map out an action plan, including alternatives and the reasons for them.

Reproduced from Walker, S. and Thurston, C. *Safeguarding Children and Young People* (RHP, 2006) ISBN: 1-903855-90-4. www.russellhouse.co.uk

Activity 6.3

Can you think of instances of interventions which should not be attempted unless adequate resources were secured in advance?

Reproduced from Walker, S. and Thurston, C. *Safeguarding Children and Young People* (RHP, 2006) ISBN: 1-903855-90-4. www.russellhouse.co.uk

Activity 6.4

Can you think of other examples in your own experience of complex pieces of work which should not be undertaken unless an appropriate amount of time is made available?

Reproduced from Walker, S. and Thurston, C. *Safeguarding Children and Young People* (RHP, 2006) ISBN: 1-903855-90-4. www.russellhouse.co.uk

Activity 7.1

Reflect on the specific risk taking behaviours the young people you work with may experience.

Is there any *common behavioural link to the geographical location or environment*?

Reproduced from Walker, S. and Thurston, C. *Safeguarding Children and Young People* (RHP, 2006) ISBN: 1-903855-90-4. www.russellhouse.co.uk

Activity 7.2

What specific issues and characteristics relate to the young people you work with that leads them to take risks?

How is this viewed by the rest of the local community?

Reproduced from Walker, S. and Thurston, C. *Safeguarding Children and Young People* (RHP, 2006) ISBN: 1-903855-90-4. www.russellhouse.co.uk

Activity 7.3

What specific assessment issues have to be considered when exploring with the young person in your area of practice their move to adult services?

Would there be further issues for other agencies to explore that you have not included?

Reproduced from Walker, S. and Thurston, C. *Safeguarding Children and Young People* (RHP, 2006) ISBN: 1-903855-90-4. www.russellhouse.co.uk

Activity 7.4

Using the guidelines on page 103 reflect upon how you can utilise them with the young people you work with.

What other elements may need to be added for your service?

Reproduced from Walker, S. and Thurston, C. *Safeguarding Children and Young People* (RHP, 2006) ISBN: 1-903855-90-4. www.russellhouse.co.uk

Activity 8.1

Consider the role of your agency in empowerment and socially inclusive practice. Do you recognise practices consistent with that role? List three changes to your practice that aspire to empower service users.

Reproduced from Walker, S. and Thurston, C. *Safeguarding Children and Young People* (RHP, 2006) ISBN: 1-903855-90-4. www.russellhouse.co.uk

Activity 8.2

What could you do personally to translate policy guidance into effective practice with black and ethnic minority families?

Reproduced from Walker, S. and Thurston, C. *Safeguarding Children and Young People* (RHP, 2006) ISBN: 1-903855-90-4. www.russellhouse.co.uk

Activity 8.3

In what ways do you think that the safeguarding guidance does not achieve its aims in relation to helping you meet the needs of disabled children and their families?

Reproduced from Walker, S. and Thurston, C. *Safeguarding Children and Young People* (RHP, 2006) ISBN: 1-903855-90-4. www.russellhouse.co.uk

Activity 8.4

Write a paragraph describing how you think working in partnership with service users can help to integrate the requirements of both care and control. In doing this you might find it helpful to briefly re-read the section on the social construction of risk in Chapter 5 (page 73).

Reproduced from Walker, S. and Thurston, C. *Safeguarding Children and Young People* (RHP, 2006) ISBN: 1-903855-90-4. www.russellhouse.co.uk

Activity 9.1

Arrange to meet with a colleague from another agency to discuss a recent review at which you were both present. Consider whether the review fulfilled its purpose and if not what you can both do differently in future. Be honest.

Reproduced from Walker, S. and Thurston, C. *Safeguarding Children and Young People* (RHP, 2006) ISBN: 1-903855-90-4. www.russellhouse.co.uk

Activity 9.2

In your next team, staff meeting or professional consultation set aside some time to design ways to involve children and young people in more meaningful ways in reviews about their safety.

Reproduced from Walker, S. and Thurston, C. *Safeguarding Children and Young People* (RHP, 2006)
ISBN: 1-903855-90-4. www.russellhouse.co.uk

Activity 9.3

Reflect on the above and draw up a list of the skills and resources you personally need to improve to enable you to maintain a focus on the safety of the child as well as insight into the feelings of parents during reviews

Reproduced from Walker, S. and Thurston, C. *Safeguarding Children and Young People* (RHP, 2006)
ISBN: 1-903855-90-4. www.russellhouse.co.uk

Activity 9.4

The case study on pages 130 and 131 gives an example where partnership appears fraught with difficulties and may appear unachievable. You have just been told to review this case and transfer it to another area because the family are moving. Think about how you would try to work in partnership with the family while conveying your concerns to other professionals.

Reproduced from Walker, S. and Thurston, C. *Safeguarding Children and Young People* (RHP, 2006)
ISBN: 1-903855-90-4. www.russellhouse.co.uk